accla

for *a third testament*

WILLIAM F. BUCKLEY, JR.

Muggeridge was a most eloquent lay apostle of Christianity...
and a journalist with few, if any, peers.

THOMAS HOWARD

SAINT JOHN'S SEMINARY, MANCHESTER, MA

Both a wag and a lethally shrewd observer of history and hum-
bug, Muggeridge brings alive seven colossi of the Western intellectual tradition – and shows us that the majority of them,
ironically, are in fact quite counter-traditional. The result is a
very great treasure, and a highly recommended read.

PETER KREEFT

BOSTON COLLEGE

After Chesterton, Lewis, and Tolkien, there is no one I would
rather read than Muggeridge. A Johnny-come-lately convert
to Christianity, he is also a great wordsmith, and that rarity –
an intellectual who is clever and funny, yet incapable of dis-
honesty.

FREDERICA MATHEWES-GREEN

BELIEFNET COLUMNIST AND AUTHOR,
"THE ILLUMINED HEART"

God has always written his stories in the lives of those who
love him, even those whose love is marked by struggle. In this
marvelous short book we encounter seven of those incarnate

stories, written by an eighth. Plough is to be congratulated on returning this classic to print.

A Third Testament reveals the gifts that made "St. Mug" such an effective apologist for the Christian way in his latter days. This scintillating little book continues to provoke, charm, and persuade.

In times like these, that try our souls, everyone needs a book like this: it is readable, stimulating, and substantive. It leaves you with the same feeling you have after a wonderful meal – though in this case, of course, the feeling lasts longer.

This classic occupies a spot on my shelf of favorite books.

Muggeridge was a true prophet of the 20th Century…a voice crying in the wilderness.

a third testament

a third testament

MALCOLM MUGGERIDGE

A modern pilgrim explores the spiritual wanderings of Augustine, Blake, Pascal, Tolstoy, Bonhoeffer, Kierkegaard, and Dostoevsky

ORBIS BOOKS
Maryknoll, New York 10545

Second Printing, March 2007

Founded in 1970, Orbis Books endeavors to publish works that enlighten the mind, nourish the spirit, and challenge the conscience. The publishing arm of the Maryknoll Fathers and Brothers, Orbis seeks to explore the global dimensions of the Christian faith and mission, to invite dialogue with diverse cultures and religious traditions, and to serve the cause of reconciliation and peace. The books published reflect the views of their authors and do not represent the official position of the Maryknoll Society. To learn more about Maryknoll and Orbis Books, please visit our website at www.maryknoll.org.

Copyright © 1976 by Little, Brown, & Co. (Canada) Limited. Dostoevsky chapter and new foreword copyright © 1983 by Malcolm Muggeridge. This edition published 2002 by the Plough Publishing House of the Bruderhof Foundation.

Published in 2004 by Orbis Books, Maryknoll, NY 10545-0308, by arrangement with Little, Brown and Company, Inc., New York, NY.

Manufactured in the United States of America

The Library of Congress has catalogued the original edition as follows:

Muggeridge, Malcolm, 1903-
    A third testament: a modern pilgrim explores the spiritual wanderings of Augustine, Blake, Pascal, Tolstoy, Bonhoeffer, Kierkegaard, and Dostoevsky/Malcolm Muggeridge.
        xxx, 172p.; 19cm.
ISBN 0-87486-921-8 (pbk.: alk. paper)
1. Augustine, Saint, Bishop of Hippo. 2. Pascal, Blaise, 1623-1662.
3. Blake, William, 1757-1827—Religion. 4. Kierkegaard, Søren, 1813-1855.
5. Dostoevsky, Fyodor, 1821-1881. 6. Tolstoy, Leo, graf, 1828-1910. 7.
Bonhoeffer, Dietrich, 1906-1945. 1. Title.
    BR1700.3.M83 2002
    270'.092'2—dc21

                                                        2002001540

ORBIS/ISBN 1-57075-532-9

contents

introduction

No, no, no! Come, let's away to prison:
We two alone will sing like birds i' the cage...
And take upon's the mystery of things
As if we were God's spies.

King Lear

It often happens that the reason for doing something only
emerges clearly after it has been done, conscious intent and
all the various practicalities which go therewith being but
the tip of an iceberg of unconscious intent. In any case, as
has often been pointed out, time itself is a continuum, and
not divisible into past, present and future tenses. Thus, it
was only after the completion of the series of television
programs whose scripts are here collected, when I was
asked to explain why I had chosen Saint Augustine, Blaise
Pascal, William Blake, Søren Kierkegaard, Fyodor Dostoevsky, Leo Tolstoy and Dietrich Bonhoeffer to be their
subjects, that I fully grasped the theme to which they all
belonged. Previously, I had seen them singly and separately as seven characters in search of God, and as such of

great interest, and a formative influence in my own thinking and questing.

Considering them as a group, it became clear to me that, although they were all quintessentially men of their time, they had a special role in common, which was none other than to relate their time to eternity. This has to be done every so often; otherwise, when the lure of self-sufficiency proves too strong, or despair too overwhelming, we forget that men need to be called back to God to rediscover humility and with it, hope. In the case of the Old Testament Jews, it was the prophets who thus called them back to God — and when were there more powerful and poetic voices than theirs? Then came the New Testament, which is concerned with how God, through the Incarnation, became His own prophet. Nor was even that the end of prophets and testaments. Between the fantasies of the ego and the truth of love, between the darkness of the will and the light of the imagination, there will always be the need for a bridge and a prophetic voice calling on us to cross it. This is what my seven seekers after God were destined to provide, each in his own way and in relation to his own time.

So I came to see them as God's spies, posted in actual or potential enemy-occupied territory, the enemy being, of course, in this particular case, the Devil. As it happens I was myself involved in espionage operations in the Sec-

ond World War, when I served with MI6, the wartime
version of the British Secret Service, or SIS. We had, for
instance, what were known as stay-behind agents in Ger-
man-occupied France, who were required to lie low until
circumstances arose in which they could make themselves useful by collecting and transmitting intelligence,
or organizing sabotage. While they were waiting to be
activated, it was essential that they should make themselves inconspicuous by merging into the social and political scene, and, in their opinions and attitudes, echoing
the current consensus. Thus, it would be appropriate for
a stay-behind agent posted in, say, Vichy France, to be
ostensibly Pétainist in politics, Catholic in religion, and
bourgeois in way of life, eschewing any association with
resistance organizations and, equally, the more fervid
pro-Nazi ones. By this means he might hope to establish
himself as a loyal supporter of Marshal Pétain, and so,
when the time came, be the better placed to act effectively
on behalf of the belligerent Gaullists and their Anglo-
American allies.

Those who direct our intelligence services are not
blessed with the insights and vision of God – though they
are sometimes prone to suppose so. Nor are our human
calamities in God's eyes what they seem to be in ours.
There is no imagery that can convey even the similitude of
God, let alone forecast His purposes; to know Him at all

we are beholden to the great mercy of the Incarnation. Even so, in considering the place of a Saint Augustine in history, it is possible to see his role as that of a stay-behind agent posted by a celestial spymaster in a collapsing Roman Empire with a brief to promote the Church's survival as custodian of the Christian revelation. Certainly, no one could have been better qualified for such a role than the famous Bishop of Hippo, ardent, as he was, for Roman civilization as only a North African could be, and ardent for Catholic orthodoxy as only a convert and sometime Manichean heretic could be.* His worldly credentials were impeccable – a highly successful professorship of rhetoric at Milan University, which in his regenerate days he called his Chair of Lies, friends and acquaintances in the highest circles and occasional speech-writing jobs for the Emperor himself. As for his *pièces justificatives,* as the French police call supporting documents, who could ask for anything better than his *Confessions*, the first great autobiography and still reckoned among the greatest, and his *City of God,* which laid down the guidelines for Christians, first to survive, and then to set about building a new great civilization to be known as Christendom?

When Augustine came to die, the barbarians were al-

---

*Manicheism, to which Augustine adhered for some nine years before his conversion, was based on the notion of an eternal conflict between light and darkness. Its followers were expected to practice extreme asceticism.

ready at the gates of Hippo, and were pillaging and burning the city while his body lay in his basilica awaiting burial. His services on behalf of his Church, however, by no means ended with his life, but continued through the succeeding Dark and Middle Ages, defining and strengthening the faith he had so cherished, thereby facilitating its movement westward to leave in its train great cathedrals like Chartres to mark its progress.

> If St. Augustine appeared today, and had as little authority as his defenders, he would achieve nothing. God guided His Church well by sending him earlier, and investing him with the proper degree of authority.

Thus wrote Blaise Pascal some ten centuries after Augustine's death. By that time new dangers were threatening. The great torrent of creativity released by Christianity now looked as if it were overflowing its banks, sweeping aside the dikes and dams designed to hold it back. In place of the Cloud of Unknowing between God and us, a Cloud of Knowing was gathering; now, the threat was of light, not darkness – a dazzling, blinding light. This time God's finger pointed inexorably at Pascal himself. He it was who would be required to counteract a two-fold attack: on the one hand, a clamor for self-indulgence, freedom from all restraint, license to, in his own words, "lick the earth"; and, on the other, the first crazy rumblings of godless men of science, so blown up with pride in their own achievements and the staggering potentialities thereby opened up, that they were beginning to think they were gods themselves, capable of shaping their own destiny and creating a kingdom of heaven on earth.

Pascal's credentials as God's spy in these particular circumstances were no less impeccable than Augustine's had been in the situation created by the fall of Rome. Ostensibly, he was supremely a man of his time; by virtue of his mathematical and scientific attainments in the same class as a Newton, as a thinker on equal terms with a Descartes, and as a polemicist and stylist equipped to aim effective barbs at a Montaigne. As a Jansenist* sympathizer, Pascal was deep in the controversies raised by the Reformation, and came within an ace of being excommunicated – something, incidentally, liable to happen to God's spies at all times, whether at the hands of the Inquisition, political police, or, the latest variant, the Media Pundits. His *Lettres provinciales*, venomously attacking the time-serving Jesuits, were by universal consent a masterpiece of demolition and irony, and all in all there seemed every reason for regarding him as an outstanding and characteristic product

---

*Jansenism, a heresy derived from the Augustinianism of Cornelius Jansen, in Pascal's time Bishop of Ypres. It holds that grace is irresistible, and has therefore been regarded as deterministic and in line with Calvinism. Its followers, who included the religious of Port Royal, among them Pascal's sister Jacqueline, practiced extreme asceticism.

of the Renaissance and a harbinger of the Enlightenment to come.

Yet all this amounted only to what Pascal called "distractions," intended, as he put it, "to amuse us and bring us imperceptibly to death." The divine briefing had already taken place, and he knew just what he had to do, which was no less than to use every scrap of knowledge he had acquired, his scientific explorations and experimentations, all the gifts of the intellect and the imagination God had endowed him with, to produce his great masterpiece, his superb apologia for the Christian faith itself, posthumously named his *Pensées*. Furthermore, by a signal grace, due to his early death at thirty-nine, this splendid exercise in faith at its most durable and thought at its most perceptive, was left behind him in the form of notes on scraps of paper rather than the long, conscientiously worked over, and possibly tedious, treatise he had envisaged.

The notes, revealing, as they do, the working of his brilliant mind, have been uniquely effective in their impact; personnel bombs exploding unpredictably instead of with a single devastating blast. Furthermore, the impossible task of putting the notes together in the order Pascal may be presumed to have intended has kept scholars busy who might otherwise have turned their attention to form-criticism and reinterpreting, rather than just rearranging, what

Pascal wrote. If only some similarly blameless exercise had occupied contemporary biblical scholarship, especially New Testament commentators, the Bultmanns and Kungs and Robinsons, what a blessed deliverance that would have been! It was surely significant that Pascal's worldly achievements should have included inventing the computer, which has become twentieth century man's topmost graven image, before which he readily prostrates himself, and whose cryptic utterances he receives like Delphic oracles. Pascal's services as God's spy were correspondingly illustrious – no less than the exposition and celebration of the true Christian faith in words so luminous that they have continued to shine with their own inner light ever since, like an El Greco portrait.

> I turn my eyes to the Schools & Universities
>   of Europe
> And there behold the Loom of Locke,
>   whose Woof rages dire,
> Wash'd by the Water-wheels of Newton:
>   black the cloth
> In heavy wreathes folds over every Nation:
>   cruel Works
> Of many Wheels I view, wheel without
>   wheel, with cogs tyrannic
> Moving by compulsion each other, not as
>   those in Eden, which,

Wheel within Wheel, in freedom revolve in
harmony & peace.

These lines from William Blake's *Jerusalem* were written
about a century and a half after the *Pensées,* and in Blake's
inimitable way convey a sense similar to Pascal's that
knowledge is but a vast cul-de-sac, and the technology derived from it a dread servitude — cogs tyrannic moving by
compulsion instead of revolving in harmony and in peace
as in Eden. No two human beings could have been more
different in their backgrounds and pursuits, in their social
position and upbringing, and in the times in which they
lived, than Blake and Pascal. Yet they stood side by side in
their common awareness of the enormous dangers arising
from man's venturing into the Cloud of Knowing. Pascal
reached the conclusion that the only serious quest here on
earth was for God, and that the way to Him was chartered
in the Old Testament, sign-posted in the New, and illumined by faith. Blake likewise was insistent that only the
imagination was capable of grasping what life was about,
and he never tired of belaboring the ideologues of the age,
like Rousseau and Voltaire and Newton, or of pouring
scorn on the contemporary wisdom — for instance, Locke
on *Human Understanding* and Bacon on the *Advancement
of Learning.*

Only God would have dared to recruit so strange, inspired and erratic a person as Blake to sit out on His behalf the tumultuous years and aftermath of the French Revolution and its literary and artistic equivalent, the romantic movement. Among many of his contemporaries he passed for being mad, and in his ways and statements was so incalculable and eccentric as to be what, in human terms, is called a security risk. God, however, sees further in selecting His stay-behind agents than mortal spymasters do, and knew that His arch advocate of exuberance and excess would make of Jesus' gospel of love and self-abnegation a bright rainbow shining across a stormy sky, keeping alive the hope of deliverance from dark satanic mills of every variety, and all their lies and pollution.

Like Pascal, Blake was a man of his time; temperamentally a revolutionary himself, who rejoiced when the Revolution happened, wore the red cap of the Liberty Boys in the streets of London until the Reign of Terror led him to lay it aside, and frequented the table of Joseph Johnson, the publisher, where he met such revolutionary luminaries as William Godwin and Tom Paine, not to mention Joseph Priestly, the discoverer of oxygen, whom he immortalized as Inflammable Gas the Wind-Finder. He also had a passing relationship with Mary Wollstonecraft, known as the hyena in petticoats, who fulfilled his notion of Fearful Symmetry by becoming the wife Godwin deserved, and producing in their daughter Mary, the wife Shelley deserved.

Blake also belonged temperamentally to the romantic movement. Indeed, he may be said to have ushered it in with his glowing verses and paintings, which owed nothing to any fashion or school, and which many consider, as I do, to be its finest product. These writings and pictures remain in all their beauty and spiritual awareness to offset the tawdry offerings of later romantic artists and poets, all moving towards total mindlessness and incoherence – a Devil's Logos whereby the Word became flesh to dwell among us, graceless and full of lies.

Over in Denmark, of all places, another prophetic voice was to be raised – Søren Kierkegaard's – to echo, and project still further into the future, Pascal's and Blake's. Kierkegaard knew and admired Pascal's writings, but though his life overlapped with Blake's (he was fourteen when Blake died), it is extremely improbable that he ever heard tell of him. What he and Blake had in common was a detestation of the sort of materialist-collectivist society they saw coming to pass around them, and an uncanny awareness of the sinister potentialities of science. They were even alike in their oddity, which set them apart from their contemporaries; in their resolute determination to go their own way without making concessions to the collectivity. Seeing them in terms of their predecessors, the Hebrew prophets, Blake was Isaiah and Kierkegaard, Amos; both their voices being raised in warning against the wrath to come if men decided to dispense with God and establish His Kingdom here on earth, with appropriate laws and morality and ecclesiastical establishments.

Of all God's spies, a motley enough crew anyway, Kierkegaard is surely one of the weirdest. Interminably wandering about the streets of Copenhagen, one trouser leg shorter than the other, he had the people in the cafés nudging one another and exchanging significant nods and winks as he passed by. How could he possibly have understood in advance, as he did, the great hoax of universal-suffrage democracy, so that in Westminster or on Capitol Hill it is his sharp sayings that come to mind rather than Jefferson's, Bagehot's, or Bryce's ponderously structured ones? How could his impish mind have reached out, as it did, into the newsrooms, the radio and television studios, the communications satellites keeping the *muʒak* and *newʒak* going round the world and round the clock? How to have foreseen so clearly those voices canting slogans in unison, on campuses, in Red Square, wherever uniformity was masquerading as unanimity? Or, take this: "A passionate, tumultuous age will overthrow everything, pull everything down; but a revolutionary age that is at the same time reflective and passionless leaves everything standing but cunningly empties it of significance." What a perfect description of the revolutionary happenings now, which take place silently, invisibly, with the media lulling everyone to sleep, until the people awaken – if they ever do – to find that the Honorable and Right Honorable Members going in and out of the Aye and No lobbies are ghosts voting for and against nothing; that the vested priests at the high altar are praying to no one about nothing, and dispensing wine and wafers lifeless as stale yeast; that the currency notes being printed at the Mint have lost their value before they come off the presses, as the words dispatched to the composing room have lost their meaning before they are printed. In such circumstances, what is the need for a revolution? It would be like blitzing Pompei – something that actually happened in the Italian campaign in the Second World War, though nobody noticed. Such insights are not of this world; at the non-stop treason trial which is history, Kierkegaard stands convicted of working as an undercover agent for God.

Dostoevsky, notoriously a Slavophile, Christian, monarchist, and inveterate anti-Marxist, falls perfectly into the category of God's Spies; he foresaw with uncanny clarity how the terrible pride and dynamism of godless men seeking to construct an earthly paradise would infallibly prove destructive to themselves, their fellow human beings, and ultimately to what we still call Christendom.

When I was first in Russia, in 1932, Dostoevsky was still anathema because of his essentially religious view of life, as expressed in *The Idiot* and *The Brothers Karamazov*, and because of his detestation of revolutionaries and their ideologies, especially Marxism, as expressed in *The Devils*. His grave in St. Petersburg, when I visited it, was neglected and difficult to find, and his books, though not specifically banned, were unobtainable. In any case, Lenin had savagely attacked Dostoevsky and his writings, which at that time precluded any attempt to re-establish his reputation. Especially offensive in the climate of the Soviet regime was the famous speech he delivered in 1880, the year before he died, on the occasion of the unveiling of the Pushkin statue in Moscow. In the speech, Dostoevsky lambasted the revolutionary and nihilistic views which, he claimed, came into Russia from the West. He spoke in exalted mystical terms of Russia's great destiny to unite mankind in a brotherhood based on Christian love as the antidote to power rather than on power as the antidote to the inequality, the injustice, the oppression under which the poor everywhere labored.

At the time the speech was rapturously received. Bringing it into my commentary necessitated quoting words from it which, uttered in Russian and by a Soviet citizen, would lead straight to the Gulag Archipelago. Equipped with a radio mic, and speaking these words as I walked along a crowded Moscow street, gave me a kind of ecstasy such as I have rarely experienced. None of the passersby heard what I was saying or would have understood it if they had; in their eyes I was just a foreigner for some reason given to muttering to himself. Yet nonetheless, as I conjured up in my mind the extraordinary response to Dostoevsky's words when he spoke them, somehow I knew without any shadow of doubt that his vision of Christ's gospel of love triumphing over Marx's gospel of power was certain, ultimately, to be fulfilled.

We filmed the Dostoevsky program in Russia just when the tide had turned, and he had become acceptable. In preparation for the celebration of the centenary of his death, a large edition of his collected works had been published and proved enormously popular. It was fascinating to observe how Dostoevsky's books, products of a mind diametrically opposed to everything the Soviet regime stood for, could, by virtue of an amazing exercise in ideological gymnastics, be molded into seeming compatible with the current Party Line – rather like discovering in Gandhi's life and writings another Genghis Khan, or in Mussolini a reincarnation of St. Francis of Assisi.

The case of Tolstoy in my little galaxy of God's spies is particularly interesting, if only because he is still, as it were, *en poste*, so that his performance is open to scrutiny by a discerning eye. This was very obvious while we were

filming the program on Tolstoy in Russia at places associated with him – his Moscow home, his country estate
Yasnaya Polyana, near Tula, and the obscure little railway station at Astapova where he died. In some degree I
had been prepared for the experience when I interviewed
for BBC television a Russian writer named Anatoly
Kuznetsov who had defected and sought asylum in England. In talking with him, I became aware that his way
of looking at life had distinct Christian undertones.
When I mentioned this, he told me that soon after he was
born his Ukrainian grandmother had arranged for him to
be secretly baptized. Even so, I put it to him, he could
scarcely have had a Christian upbringing under the mili-
tantly godless Soviet regime. What about the Gospels,
for instance? They, surely, were unavailable. Yes, he said,
that was so, and then went on to deliver himself of a
memorable remark – namely, that Stalin had made a very
great mistake in not banning the works of Tolstoy and
Dostoevsky.

I saw the point, of course, and continued to marvel at
the extraordinary chance – if chance it was – whereby
the works of the two greatest Christian writers of modern times should have continued to circulate in the
world's first avowedly atheistic state. After all, between
them they cover the whole ground, from Tolstoy's splen-
didly lucid commentaries on the New Testament, his ac-

count of his conversion in his *Confession*, as well as his short stories, each one a parable of consummate artistry, to Dostoevsky's devastatingly penetrating exposition of sin and suffering and redemption. Supposing one were asked to name the two books best calculated to give an unbeliever today a clear notion of what Christianity is about, could one hope to do better than *Resurrection* and *The Brothers Karamazov*? Kuznetsov was undoubtedly correct in his supposition that by allowing the circulation of Tolstoy's and Dostoevsky's works, Stalin unwittingly counteracted in the most effective way possible all the efforts of the Soviet propaganda machine, with its anti-God museums and equivalent publications and exhortations and scientific mumbo-jumbo, to extirpate the practice, and even the memory, of the Christian religion among the Russian people.

Holding forth in front of a camera is not an activity that in the ordinary way I find particularly congenial, but somehow, in the light of the thoughts my conversation with Kuznetsov had conjured up, I found our filming expedition to the Soviet Union in search of Tolstoy quite entrancing. This was especially true of the days we spent at Yasnaya Polyana, which, in the perfect autumn weather, seemed an enchanted place. Standing by Tolstoy's grave, looking over the ravine where as a child he had believed the green stick was hidden which had carved on it the secret of everlasting happiness, and speaking there of the beautiful way he had written about the New Testament, in shining words, so clear and telling that they might have been specially intended for minds otherwise uninformed or deliberately closed-up on the subject; speaking, too, of his inveterate distrust of power and of those who exercised it, however seemingly well-disposed their intentions, I felt uplifted, myself. My audience, it is true, was only a gaping camera, with, gathered round it, our own *équipe*, along with some Russians attached to us for one purpose and another, but I seemed to catch a glimpse of another presence, lurking among the silver birches he had planted a century before, bearded, high-booted and belted, in his familiar peasant's blouse. Could it be…was it possible that he was favoring me with a distinctively mischievous wink?

Immediately following our filming by Tolstoy's grave, I was due to be interviewed myself by the local Tula television station. My interviewer, an agreeable individual in leather trousers, was already standing by, and told me that he proposed to put to me only one question – Why did I admire Tolstoy? – which seemed fair enough. While I was walking up and down thinking of what I should say, the Russian who was to act as interpreter fell into step beside me, and, in a soft persuasive voice, with, as it seemed to me, undertones of ridicule, remarked that

Tolstoy had been a great pacifist, had he not? I agreed that he had, though without adding that thereby he had earned the unbounded contempt of Lenin. In that case, the interpreter went on, it would be greatly appreciated if I were to point out that Mr. Brezhnev's policy of détente might be regarded as the fulfillment of Tolstoy's pacifism.

It was difficult to keep a straight face, but out of consideration for the interpreter I contented myself with saying that Mr. Brezhnev's policy of détente was to do with diplomacy, a heavily-mined field into which I should not care to venture. There the matter rested, and when I came to answer the single question of why I admired Tolstoy I stuck to my three points – his greatness as a writer, his unique quality as a spokesman for Christ, and his abiding distrust of governments, whatever their complexion and ostensible objectives. No words I have ever uttered, I think, gave me more satisfaction than these, even though I felt sure they would never be transmitted. It was a kind of ecstasy to be speaking them in those circumstances and in that place. In the event, as I anticipated, all that appeared on the television screen was some mute footage of us filming at Yasnaya Polyana, but I felt that what I had said would also linger on among the silver birch trees in some mysterious way.

In Moscow we filmed in front of the headquarters of the Soviet Writers Union. The house was the one Tolstoy had used for the residence of the Rostov family in *War and Peace*, and a large statue of him dominates the façade. Again, as at Yasnaya Polyana, I was conscious of Tolstoy's presence. Looking up at his statue – artistically, not particularly good, but still the likeness sufficed – I saw in his bronze face what the Russian writer Maxim Gorky had so well described: something everlasting, near at hand and faraway, divinely earthy and innocently old.

There remains Dietrich Bonhoeffer, who, for me, does not fit into the role of God's spy as clearly and succinctly as the others, doubtless because he is the nearest to us in time. God's spies, by the nature of the case, require to be seen in a certain perspective to be fully understood and appreciated. Bonhoeffer continues to be enmeshed in the present, and so to some extent partakes of its uncertainties and equivocations. For instance, he took his great decision to join the conspiracy to kill Adolf Hitler even though he recognized that so doing might be a mortal sin. In other words, he considered that delivering Germany from the Nazi regime was more important even than saving his own soul. We who have seen the consequences of Germany's deliverance from Hitler may well question Bonhoeffer's decision; but he was spared any such agonizing doubts by his martyrdom just before Germany's final defeat.

It is interesting to me that in London Simone Weil, another of God's spies, working with the Gaullists and becoming increasingly doubtful about what the forthcoming *soi-disant* liberation of France was going to amount to in terms of her values, was likewise spared the unedifying spectacle of Charles De Gaulle's Fifth Republic, as Bonhoeffer was that of Germany's Federal Republic. In her case, admittedly, her death in 1943 can be regarded as in some degree self-inflicted, in that its ostensible cause was her refusal to eat. The effect, however, was the same as Bonhoeffer's martyrdom – that she did not live to see the hollowness of the Allied victory she had so passionately hoped for and believed in. And how greatly she would have preferred to die like Bonhoeffer on a Nazi scaffold to dying of malnutrition in a Kent hospital!

Standing on the Berlin Wall I tried to imagine what would have been Bonhoeffer's feelings if, instead of being martyred, he had lived on into post-war divided Germany. Eastwards, I could see the familiar scene of desolation and oppression, the bedraggled houses, the empty shops, the somehow muted traffic and people in the streets; westwards, the other sort of desolation and oppression, equally familiar, the gleaming neon and glass, the exhortations to spend and to consume, the banks for churches and the erotica for dreams. The pursuit of power versus the pursuit of happiness, black-and-white television versus color, the clenched fist versus the raised phallus, guns before butter and butter before guns. And in between, the no-man's land or limbo of vigilant sentries on watch-towers, dogs and land-mines and armed patrols. Was there anything here to risk eternal damnation for, or for that matter to live for? The strip-tease joints and the garish posters announcing the mighty achievements of the triumphant German proletariat, equally fantasy. Plastic flesh and fraudulent statistics – where's the difference? Perhaps, after all, the limbo is the place, lurking among the land-mines.

Bonhoeffer's active service as God's spy ends, then, with an unanswered question. Maybe his perfect serenity as he went to his execution was partly due to the fact that now he would never have to answer it – at least not in this world. Meanwhile, we may be sure that other spies have been briefed and posted. It would be foolish even to speculate on their identity and whereabouts. As has already been said, the first duty of a stay-behind agent is to take on the coloration of the contemporary scene. One thing is certain, though: whoever and wherever they may be, great services will be required of them and great dangers encompass them.

saint augustine

---

354 – 430 A.D.

When at the beginning of the fifth century A.D. Rome was sacked, Augustine was at the height of his fame as the Bishop of Hippo in North Africa. Confronted with the dissolution of the Roman Empire, like a latter-day Noah, he was constrained to construct an ark, in his case Orthodoxy, wherein his Church could survive through the dark days that lay ahead.

Thanks largely to Augustine, the light of the New Testament did not go out with Rome's but remained amidst the debris of the fallen empire to light the way to another civilization, Christendom, whose legatees we are.

It was as though he had been specially groomed for the task. Tempered in the fires of his own sensuality, toughened by his arduous explorations of the heresies of the age, he was a master of words written and spoken, which he offered in God's service, first asking that God would give him the wherewithal to offer.

In Augustine's eyes Rome stood at the very pinnacle of history. He saw it as the secular state carried to the highest degree of perfection, providing the only tolerable framework of life for mankind. Its disappearance from the human scene, if so unthinkable a catastrophe were to happen, would leave behind not other, alternative civilizations, but a vacuum, a darkness.

Augustine's own North Africa partook of this glory. The city of Carthage was a little Rome. The abundant harvests, the flourishing cities and ports, the entertainments and spectacles, all signified participation in the Roman Empire, which to Augustine was the whole world.

Augustine was born in the year 354, some forty years after Christianity had become the acknowledged religion of the Roman Empire under Constantine. His birthplace was in a hilly district of North Africa, the Roman province then known as Numidia, in one of the many small towns which were scattered about what was then a rich and luxuriant countryside.

His father, Patricius, belonged to the middle classes and was reasonably well off except that he was a victim of the very excessive taxation which characterized those troubled years. He was a wealthy man who remained a pagan till the end of his life, when he was belatedly baptized a Christian. Augustine's mother Monica, on the other hand, was a Christian of tremendous piety. Without any question, her devotions and meditations were conducive to Augustine not fulfilling his father's purpose and becoming a successful lawyer or civil servant, but, as she hoped, dedicating his life to the service of Christ and the Church. She made him a saint and his sanctity resulted, in due course, in her being canonized.

His studies went easily. He excelled and quite soon became a teacher of rhetoric – a rather empty and pretentious discipline which in those days was very highly regarded, rather as sociology is today. Looking back on his profession, he contemptuously called it being a vendor of words. Alas, my own trade!

By the end of the fourth century the decadence which had afflicted Rome had spread to the northern African provinces, especially to the great port and metropolis of Carthage, at whose university Augustine studied and later taught. Thence he transferred to Rome because he said he found the Carthage students too turbulent – a very contemporary touch.

To a provincial like young Augustine, the Mediterranean would have seemed like the gateway to the larger world of Rome. After all, he was a very ambitious man, and in his time, as in ours, eminence as a man of letters or as an academic could lead to positions of great power and responsibility.

Also, I think, he wanted to escape from the watchful eye of his mother, Monica, and indulge freely in what Pascal would later call "licking the earth," and Augustine himself, after his conversion, would describe as "scratching the itching sore of lust." So, to avoid the pain and embarrassment of saying goodbye to his mother, one night he slipped away across the sea, taking with him his mistress and their son, Adeodatus. It was on any showing a very unkind thing to do and afterwards his contrition for it was great.

In Rome he easily consorted with some of the most famous figures of the time, and was appointed to the Chair of Rhetoric in Milan. The appointment brought him into contact with the Imperial Court, and – even more important, from the point of view of his subsequent career – with the famous and saintly Bishop Ambrose. So, at the age of thirty, he had reached the summit of a career with a dazzling prospect before him. But somehow, he remained totally unsatisfied. He called his university appointment his "chair of lies," knowing in his heart that God had some other purpose for him and that, try as he might, he would never be able to escape his true calling.

Roman games and theatre were given over to wildly expensive spectacles of violence and eroticism, like films and, increasingly, television today. To judge by the way that after his conversion Augustine never lost an opportunity of thundering against such spectacles, it is reasonable to assume that he was by no means immune to their appeal. There is also the touching story in Augustine's autobiography, the *Confessions*, of a friend who, with great effort, had managed to break an addiction to the games, was tricked into going to them, ventured to open just one eye, and was hooked again.

The pagan temples still functioned, but few attended or heeded them. The Christian churches, now under state patronage, were not strong enough to counteract, or even always to resist, the prevailing atmosphere of luxury, violence and self-indulgence. With his sensual disposition and inquiring mind, Augustine was little disposed to hold aloof, though a certain intellectual and physical fastidiousness prevented him from succumbing wholly to a way of life which would assuredly have destroyed him.

It is easier for us to get inside Augustine's unregenerate skin than perhaps it would be for any of the intervening generations. The similarity between his circumstances and ours is striking, if not to say alarming. There is the same moral vacuity, leading to the same insensate passion for new sensations and experiences; the same fatuous credulity opening the way to every kind of charlatanry and quackery from fortune telling to psychoanalysis; the same sinister combination of great wealth and pointless ostentation with appalling poverty and unheeded affliction. As Augustine wrote, "O greedy men, what will satisfy you if God Himself will not?"

We know what it is like. We also know that to a temperament as sensual and imaginative as Augustine's, sexual indulgence makes the greatest appeal precisely because it offers a kind of fraudulent ecstasy – joys that expire when the neon lights go out.

"There's nothing so powerful," he said when he was a Bishop, "in drawing the spirit of man downwards as the caresses of a woman." He was speaking from experience and I, for what it's worth, endorse his opinion.

Augustine's *Confessions* is really the first autobiography, in the modern sense of the term. For that reason we know more about him than about any other figure in antiquity. Of course, it is not just an account of his life, it is also an account of his quest for truth. So the culminating point in it, from his point of view at any rate, is his conversion. He naturally thought, as did Saint Paul, that this conversion happened at a particular moment, but actually it was the result of a long process which had begun even before he was aware of it.

Knowing his nature, Monica had hurried after her son to Milan to watch over him, and pray for his soul's redemption. Moreover, some of the friends he had made among the amusing, the cultivated and the well-born turned out to be Christians, a fact which came as something of a surprise to Augustine, who in North Africa had associated Christianity with the poor and the lowly. In Milan a great Roman administrator, like Ambrose, might renounce his career to become a bishop, and rich heiresses dispose of all their property to the Church.

It was under Ambrose's influence that Augustine began to study the scriptures, noting particularly the spiritual meaning of Old Testament stories, which had formerly made little impression on him. This played an important part in his final deliverance from the heresy of Manicheism and his ultimate conversion.

The climax of Augustine's conversion occurred in a garden in Milan and its fulfillment in another garden in the country. I think he must have loved gardens, where for him the truth stood out most clearly. First, however, there was one episode in the process leading up to his conversion which received special mention in his *Confessions:*

> My misery was complete and I remember how one day You made me realize how utterly wretched I was. I was preparing a speech in praise of the Emperor, intending that it should include a great many lies which would certainly be

applauded by an audience who knew well enough how far from the truth they were. I was greatly preoccupied by this task, my mind was feverishly busy with its harassing problems. As I walked along one of the streets of Milan, I noticed a poor beggar who must, I suppose, have had his fill of food and drink, since he was laughing and joking.

Contrasting their two conditions – his own so troubled, the beggar's so cheerful – he cried out in desperation,

Will I never cease setting my heart on shadows and following a lie?

His anguish and contrition are all too actual to me after more than forty years in the same sort of profession.

Nonetheless Augustine's mind continued to be occupied with thoughts of fame and success. He was planning to marry a rich woman, having callously sent away the mistress he had brought from North Africa, who had lived with him for fifteen years, and keeping their son, Adeodatus, on whom he doted. Then matters came to a head in the garden of the house where he lived. As he described it: "I now found myself driven by the tumult in my breast to take refuge in this garden where no one could interrupt that fierce struggle in which I was my own contestant, until it came to its conclusion."

In this mood he "suddenly heard the sing-song voice of a child in a nearby house. Whether it was the voice of a boy or a girl, I can't say but again and again it repeated the refrain, 'Take it and read it, take it and read it.'" So, he rushed to where he had left a copy of the Gospels open at Saint Paul's Epistle to the Romans and read: "Not in revelling and drunkenness, not in lust and wantonness, not in quarrels and rivalries, rather, arm yourself with the Lord Jesus Christ. Spend no more thought on nature and nature's appetites."

Augustine continued: "I had no wish to read more and no need to do so, for in an instant as I came to the end of the sentence, it was as though the light of confidence flooded into my heart and all the darkness and doubt was dispelled."

No one must suppose that this great conversion which had befallen Augustine, this light which had shone into his life and would never again leave it, had turned him away from this world. On the contrary, it made him more conscious then ever before of its joys and beauties, more aware than ever before of the terrific privilege it was to be allowed to exist in time. There is a passage that I love in the *Confessions* in which he asks "the earth itself, the winds that blow, and the whole air, and all that lives in it…'What is my God?'" Likewise he asks the sky, the moon and the stars: "What is my God?" None of these was God, he was told. He went on to speak to "all the things that are about me, all that can be admitted by the door of the senses." They, too, he was told, were not God. Then at last he understood: their beauty was all the answer they could give, and the only answer he needed to hear.

Following his conversion, Augustine set out with Monica to return to North Africa, resolving to dedicate the remaining years of his life wholly to the service of Christ. They reached the port of Ostia and were delayed there, because the Mediterranean was infested with pirates and no boats would put to sea.

How different was the Augustine who returned to North Africa from the one who had left for Rome! Now he was as avid to leave the world as he had been to plunge into it; as ardently in search of obscurity as he had once sought fame.

It was while they were waiting in Ostia that Augustine and Monica had an extraordinary, mystical experience which is described in the *Confessions* with incomparable artistry and skill. They were looking out of the window of the house in which they were staying into the courtyard below, talking together serenely and joyfully about the eternal life of the saints, which, they agreed, "no bodily pleasure, however great it might be and whatever earthly light might shed luster upon it, was worthy of comparison, or even mention." As they talked, ranging over "the whole compass of material things in their various degrees, up to the very heavens themselves," they came to survey "the eternal Wisdom, longing for it and straining for it," Augustine said, "with all the strength of our hearts."

Then they reached out and touched this eternal Wisdom, which like eternity itself is neither in the past nor the future, but just *is*. Touched it only to return, leaving, Augustine writes, "our spiritual harvest bound to it, to the sound of our own speech, in which each word has a beginning and an end; far, far different from Your Word, our Lord, Who abides in Himself forever, yet never grows old and gives new life to all things." Whoever has tried to give expression in words with a beginning and an end, to the perspectives and shape of this creation in which we live, cannot fail to feel awed that so great a writer as Augustine should suffer a like predicament.

It was after this experience that Monica told Augustine she had nothing left to live for: God had granted her every wish, now that her son was His servant, and spurned such joys as this world had to offer. Nine days later she was dead, and Augustine, leaving her mortal remains in Ostia, returned to North Africa to undertake what would become his great life's work. This was to be no less a task than to salvage from a world in ruins the Christian faith, in order that it might provide the basis for a new, splendid civilization which would grow great and then in its time, falter and fail as men, forgetting the eternal Wisdom that Monica and Augustine had glimpsed at Ostia, thought to find in their own mortal bodies the joy of living and in their own mortal minds its meaning.

In the *Confessions*, Augustine's last reference to his mother asks everyone who reads the book to remember "Monica, your servant, and with her, Patricius, her husband, who died before her, by whose bodies I was brought into this life." Through the centuries Monica has been duly remembered. As for Augustine, the rest of his life was spent in North Africa. He never crossed the sea again.

His idea was to gather a few similarly inclined friends round him and share with them a monastic life on his small estate in the hills where he was born. It was not to be. His gifts were too famous and too precious, and the need for leadership in the Church too great for him to be left in peace. As he told his congregation many years later, when he had long been a bishop, he came to Hippo – one of the many small ports along the North African coast – to see a friend whom he hoped to persuade to join him in the monastic life. Because Hippo had a bishop, Augustine went to the cathedral fearing no threat to his own privacy, but was recognized, grabbed, made a priest, and in due course a bishop.

Augustine wept when, almost under compulsion, he was first ordained a priest. Probably he would have had difficulty in explaining just what the tears were about, but one of the causes was certainly his lost dream of a life of prayer and meditation away from a troubled world. He was forty-three years old when he first mounted the cathedra as Bishop of Hippo. Thenceforth, he was endlessly involved in the duties and responsibilities of his office and the often bitter controversies of his time.

Contemplating Augustines's achievement one stands amazed. By becoming their bishop, he had in truth become the servant of his congregation – those volatile Christians of North Africa whose feelings he understood so well. Preaching to them often daily, spending his mornings adjudicating their private disputes, being available constantly to any one of them in need of help or counsel, and all the while conducting an enormous correspondence – his administrative burden was very great. Yet he was a man withdrawn from the commotion around him. Despite his great fame and involvement in his troubled times, he was somehow isolated, as though in his own inner sanctity he had achieved the monastic life he so longed for.

Gatherings of the North African hierarchy brought Augustine often to the great metropolitan church at

Carthage, where he delivered many of his greatest polemics, placing his dazzling gifts unreservedly at the service of his Church.

His public utterances and writings are full of arresting, challenging phrases, as fresh and relevant to our ears as to those who first heard them.

"This is the door of the Lord; the righteous shall enter in," was written on the lintel of a church in Numidia. However, "The man who enters," Augustine wrote:

> is bound to see drunkards, misers, tricksters, gamblers, adulterers, fornicators, people wearing amulets, assiduous clients of sorcerers, astrologers. He must be warned that the same crowds that press into the churches on Christian festivals also fill the theatres on pagan holidays...
>
> Wherever the towering mass of the theater is erected, there the foundations of Christian virtue are undermined, and while this insane expenditure gives to the sponsors a glorious result, men mock at the works of mercy...
>
> It is only charity that distinguishes the children of God from the children of the Devil. They all make the sign of the Cross, and answer "Amen" and sing Alleluia, they all go to church and build up the walls of the basilicas...
>
> Take away the barriers afforded by the laws! Men's brazen capacity to do harm, their urge to self-indulgence would rage to the full. No king in his kingdom, no general with his troops...no husband with his wife, no father with his son, could hope to stop, by any threat or punishment, the license that would follow the sheer sweet taste of sinning...

Give me a man in love; he knows what I mean. Give me one who yearns; give me one who is hungry; give me one far away in this desert, who is thirsty and sighs for the spring of the Eternal Country. Give me that sort of man; he knows what I mean. But if I speak to a cold man, he just doesn't know what I am talking about...

You are surprised that the world is losing its grip? That the world is grown old? Don't hold onto the old man, the world; don't refuse to regain your youth in Christ, who says to you: "The world is passing away; the world is losing its grip, the world is short of breath. Don't fear, thy youth shall be renewed as an eagle."

Though no one has ever been more insistent on the need for purity, equally no one has ever been less of a Puritan in the pejorative sense. Everything in creation delighted Augustine. He spoke to his congregation of the gloriously changing colors of the Mediterranean, which he had so often observed. All created things should be loved, he insisted, because God made them. The sea, the creatures, everything that is, speaks of God.

It was because Augustine was so aware of the universality of God's love and presence that he could easily communicate with all sorts and conditions of men. For instance, he once told the fishermen at Hippo:

It will not be held against you that you are ignorant against your will, but that you neglect to seek out what it is that makes you ignorant; not that you cannot bring together your wounded limbs, but that you reject Him that would heal them.

Again, like his Master, like the Gospels themselves, he used everyday imagery to make his points. As when he compared God's gifts to us to a man giving his girl a bracelet.

If she so delights in the bracelet as to forget the giver, that is an insult to him, but if she so delights in the bracelet as to love the giver more, that was what the bracelet was for...

We take for granted the slow miracle whereby water in the irrigation of a vineyard becomes wine. It is only when Christ turns water into wine, in quick motion, as it were, that we stand amazed.

And there was always the North African countryside:

When all is said and done, is there any more marvellous sight, any occasion when human reason is nearer to some sort of converse with the nature of things, than the sowing of seeds, the planting of cuttings, the transplanting of shrubs, the grafting of slips? It is as though you could question the vital force in each root and bud on what it can do, and what it cannot, and why.

So, this scintillating mind lives on in his words. Words which take account of the times in which they were spoken or written and the fears and anxieties these times generated, but which brush aside empty hopes of fashioning a better world out of mere mortal hopes for one.

> I no longer wished for a better world, because I was thinking of the whole of creation, and in the light of this clearer discernment I have come to see that, though the higher things are better than the lower, the sum of all creation is better than the higher things alone.

Augustine was fifty-six years old and in Carthage when, in the year 410, someone came and told him that Rome had been sacked. It must have been a dramatic moment in his life. Of course he knew that something of the kind was liable to happen and had prepared himself and his flock, as far as he could, for it. "Don't lose heart, brothers," he told them, "there will be an end to every earthly kingdom, and if this is actually the end now, God sees." Even so, he continued to nourish the hope, as people do when great disasters loom, that somehow it wouldn't happen.

In our time as in Augustine's we have witnessed great disasters, and we know how the flame of hope burns on. I remember well a bright August Sunday afternoon in 1940 when I stood on Camden Hill and heard the roar of the first wave of the German Luftwaffe coming over London, and thought, "No, it can't happen!"

Like many of my generation I felt that the cities of Western civilization had been morally bombed before the actual bombs began to fall. But Augustine loved and revered Rome. He saw it not just as the symbol of a great empire but as civilization itself – everything that he had admired and after which he had aspired when he was growing up and as a student in the great metropolis. Rome was art, literature, all the things he wanted to achieve; it was all that the French statesman Talleyrand would describe centuries later, when he witnessed what he thought to be the ruin of French civilization, as *douceur de vivre*, the "sweetness of life."

Augustine's first duty was to hearten his flock and prevent the panic and demoralization which the flood of refugees already beginning to arrive in North Africa from Rome might well have brought about. In a sermon delivered at the time, he compared the capture of Rome by Alaric, king of the Visigoths, with the destruction of Sodom, reminding his listeners that in the latter, biblical case, everyone had perished and the city had been eradicated by fire, never to exist again. In Rome, there were many survivors, including all who had taken refuge in the churches, Alaric himself being an Arian Christian. There had been a great deal of destruction, of course, but as Augustine pointed out, cities consist of men, not walls. Rome had been chastised but not destroyed.

"The world," he said "reels under crushing blows, the old man is shaken out, the flesh is pressed, the spirit turns to clear flowing oil."

Then he turned to the deeper question of the relations between earthly cities, like Rome, which have their day, rising and falling like everything in time, and the Heavenly City or City of God, which is everlasting. This question occupied him for the next seventeen years, almost to the end of his life, and resulted in his great work of genius, *The City of God*, which directly or indirectly influenced the thought of Christians on what they owed to God and what to Caesar through the succeeding fifteen centuries.

We live perforce, and always must, in earthly cities. They are our location, our set, with history for our script. At the same time, in all creation we are unique in being capable of envisaging a Heavenly City not susceptible to the ravages of time, existing beyond the dark jungle of the human will. As Saint Paul said, and Augustine echoed: "Here we have no continuing city, but we seek one to come."

Pursuing his theme, Augustine ranged over the whole of human history as then understood. His conclusions have lost none of their force in the light of whatever has been invented, concluded and speculated upon in the subsequent fifteen centuries:

The centuries of past history would have rolled by like empty jars if Christ had not been foretold by them…

These were the two motives which drove the Romans to their wonderful achievements: liberty, and the passion for the praise of men…

What else was there for them to love save glory? For, through glory, they desired to have a kind of life after death on the lips of those who praised them…

The Heavenly City outshines Rome, beyond comparison. There, instead of victory, is truth; instead of high rank, holiness; instead of peace, felicity; instead of life, eternity…

Take Aristotle, put him near to the Rock of Christ, and he fades away into nothingness. Who is Aristotle? When he hears the words, "Christ said," then he shakes in hell. "Pythagoras said this." "Plato said that." Put them near the Rock and compare these arrogant people with Him who was crucified!

In our fallen state, our imperfection, we can conceive perfection. Through the Incarnation, the presence of God among us in the lineaments of Man, we have a window in the walls of time which looks out on this Heavenly City. This was Augustine's profoundest conclusion, and in his great work he enshrined it imperishably, to be a comfort and a light in the dark days that lay ahead, when in the year 430, the triumphant Vandals would cross into Africa, reaching the walls of Hippo itself, as he lay dying there.

Today, the earthly city looks ever larger, to the point where it may be said to have taken over the heavenly one. Turning away from God, blown up with the arrogance generated by their fabulous success in exploring and harnessing the mechanism of life, men believe themselves to be at last in charge of their own destiny. As we survey the disastrous consequences of such an attitude, the chaos and destruction it has brought, as Augustine did the fall of Rome and its aftermath, his words on that other occasion still stand applicable, as he says, to all circumstances and conditions of men:

In its sojourn here, the Heavenly City makes use of the peace provided by the earthly city. In all that relates to the mortal nature of man it preserves and indeed seeks the concordance of human wills. It refers the earthly peace to the heavenly peace, which is truly such peace that it alone can be described as peace, for it is the highest degree of ordered and harmonious fellowship in the enjoyment of God and of another in God. When this stage is reached then there will be life, not life subject to death but life that is clearly…and assuredly life giving. There will be a body, not a body which is animal, weighing down the soul as it decays, but a spiritual body experiencing no need and subordinated in every part to the will. This is the peace that the Heavenly City has while it sojourns here in faith, and in this faith it lives a life of righteousness. To the establishing of that peace it refers all its good actions, whether they be towards God or towards one's neighbor, for the life of this City is utterly and entirely a life of fellowship.

blaise pascal

1623 – 1662

Some ten centuries after Augustine was called on to salvage the Christian Church from the ruins of the Roman Empire, Blaise Pascal, in the France of the Bourbon kings, took upon himself the task of defending the Christian faith against the arrogance and pride of those who believed they could live without God or mold His purposes to their own.

> Man is only a reed, the feeblest thing in nature, but he is a thinking reed. It is not necessary for the entire universe to take up arms in order to crush him. A vapor, a drop of water, is sufficient to kill him. But if the universe crushes him, man would still be nobler than the thing which destroys him, because he knows that he is dying, and the universe which has him at its mercy is unaware of it.

Thus did Pascal define man's superiority to nature in his great work, the *Pensées,* more than three centuries ago. If ever there was a thinking reed, it was Pascal himself. In his short life – he died when he was thirty-nine years old – he established himself as an outstanding mathematician, scientist and inventor to the point that it was considered by no means odd to compare him with Aristotle.

Under Pascal's direction, for instance, an experiment was conducted which established the existence of atmospheric pressure, thereby laying the foundations of the modern science of hydraulics. In Clermont-Ferrand, where Pascal was born, is displayed a mechanical calculator or, as he called it, a *machine arithmetique* designed on the same essential lines as today's computer. In the field of pure mathematics he is also one of the great names. An astonishing yield for one abbreviated life, any item of which would have been enough to insure that Pascal would continue to be remembered.

It is not, however, for any or all of these achievements that his fame has grown through the centuries since his death, but for something that I, like many others before me consider immeasurably greater – his sublime defense of faith as the one sure guide to reality, and of the Christian religion as showing Western man the way out of the cul-de-sac into which science must inevitably lead him.

This cul-de-sac of science has only become the more evident during the twentieth century, in which science has advanced further towards exploring and explaining the nature and mechanisms of matter than in all the rest of recorded time.

The spectacle which Pascal imagined (and we have actually seen) of our earth as a tiny revolving ball in the immensity of space, one among innumerable others great and small, has – far from turning us to God, as Pascal hoped – served rather to sharpen and intensify the idiot conceit of technologically advanced nations. This is well illustrated by the words with which U.S. President Richard Nixon greeted the first astronauts on their return from the moon in 1969:

> Let me close off with just one thing. I was thinking, you know, as you came down...it had only been eight days, just a week, a long week, that this was the greatest week in the history of the world since the Creation.

As Pascal foresaw, science, like the old pagan gods, has come to belong to man's quest for power, not truth. Man a thinking reed, yes, but his very thought processes, properly pursued, induce him to realize the limitations of thought.

For the same reason, Pascal, the most brilliant scientist of his time, denounced not the methods but the vainglorious pretensions of science – an incomparable intellect devoted to showing how very little the intellect can do.

> Know then, proud man, what a paradox you are to yourself. Humble yourself, impotent reason. Be silent, dull-witted nature, and learn from your Master your true condition, which you do not understand. Listen to God! See the Earth as a point compared with the vast circles it describes. Stand amazed that this circle itself is only a tiny point in relation to the course traced by the stars revolving in the firmament; that the whole visible world is no more than an imperceptible speck in the ample bosom of nature.

Having thus lost himself in creation's vast perspectives, man may find himself again in a God who cannot see a sparrow fall to the ground without concern, Pascal insisted. In contrast to his great contemporary, Descartes, who pursued an abstract, intellectual truth, Pascal set the personal drama of individual men seeking God. Instead of Descartes', "I think, therefore I am," Pascal said, "I look for God, therefore I have found Him."

> How few things there are which can be proved! Proofs only convince the mind. Who has ever been able to prove that tomorrow will come, and that we shall die? And what could be more generally believed?...In short, we must rely on faith when the mind has once perceived where truth lies, in order to quench our thirst and color our minds with a faith that eludes us at every moment of the day.

"Man," he concluded in the *Pensées*, "is great insofar as he realizes that he is wretched. A tree does not know its own wretchedness."

Over France in Pascal's time loomed the formidable figure of Cardinal Richelieu exercising both the power of the Church and the State. No doubt the author of the *Pensées* had Richelieu in mind when he wrote so scathingly of the pretensions of earthly authority, while at the same time being fully aware of its necessity if laws were to be enforced and order to be maintained. Like all mystics, Pascal was at heart an anarchist who nonetheless realized that as long as men needed rules to live together, they would also need power to enforce them. Like Saint Augustine, he longed for citizenship in the City of God, but meanwhile was content to accept the conditions of living in the earthly city.

It was to Richelieu that Pascal's father, Etienne Pascal, owed his appointment to high administrative positions in the service of the State, and when for a while Etienne fell out of favor and had to stay away from Paris for fear of being arrested, it was his youngest daughter, twelve-year-old Jacqueline, who successfully pleaded for her father with the Cardinal.

The children never went to school and Etienne Pascal, a true man of the Renaissance, educated them himself at home, according to carefully thought-out principles.

When Etienne was entrusted with the thankless task of collecting in Normandy the exorbitant taxes which Richelieu was bound to impose to pay for the King's wars, his son, very touchingly, worked with him night after night on his desolate accounts. It was this experience which first turned Blaise Pascal's attention to the possibility of inventing a calculating machine.

When through a chance meeting with a priest the family came into contact with the evangelical Jansenist movement within what had become, under Richelieu's dominance, a corrupt and worldly Church, they all responded. Etienne Pascal did not live to see the full involvement of his children in Jansenism, but all three of them – Jacqueline most ardently, her brother Blaise trailing along behind her, and her sister Gilberte, more sedately – remained faithful to its higher standards of piety, charity and devotion.

The Jansenist movement – named after Cornelius Jansen, a Dutch theologian and Bishop of Ypres – was strongly supported at the Abbey of Port Royal, whose Mother Superior, Mère Angélique, belonged to the Arnault family, all ardent followers of Jansen. The movement attracted such gifted, pious people, as well as aristocrats like the Duc de Roanne, a great friend of Pascal. Some of these aristocratic Jansenists became known as the *gentlemen-hermits*.

At Port Royal some of the most dramatic and decisive exchanges of Pascal's life took place with his dearly loved sister Jacqueline, who had insisted on becoming a nun at this famous convent after the death of their father.

Pascal's feelings about her renunciation of the world were mixed. At first he approved, then he opposed, and then he sourly acquiesced. At one point they were involved in a sordid row, which had Pascal shouting angrily that under no circumstances would he agree to his sister's share of their inheritance being handed over to the convent as her dowry when she took her final vows.

This particular row ended in Pascal handing over more to the convent than was required, thereby considerably reducing his income. Such rows, in my experience, are never about what they are about, and I doubt very much whether either of them really cared much about the money as such either way. Jacqueline – who was a girl of quite exceptional gifts, in some ways surpassing those of her brother, and whose dazzling attractiveness shines out across the three intervening centuries – went to the heart of the matter when she upbraided her brother by saying: "If you do not possess the strength to follow me, at least do not hold me back. Do not show yourself ungrateful to God for the grace he has given to a person whom you love."

In other words, it was envy and pride that were gnawing away at Pascal, not cupidity at all. It riled him deeply that he should go on being held a prisoner of the world that she had so gracefully and thankfully cast off – a servitude he found increasingly burdensome. In the event, of course, Pascal did turn up when Jacqueline took her final vows. She could see him through the grill in silhouette: on his knees, but still looking cross.

Actually, as I am sure she correctly divined, he was on the run, and she resolved then and there to press him hard, to make of him a Christian saint instead of merely a brilliant scientist and celebrity.

Thenceforth, in their now almost daily exchanges across the grill, it was Jacqueline who made the going. Until, as she wrote to Gilberte in September, 1654:

> He opened his heart to me in a way that could not but fill me with pity. He admitted that in the midst of his many occupations and the pleasures of the fashionable world, by which he seemed to set so much store, he was conscious of an overwhelming urge to abandon everything.

It was an important admission, but still, though he felt this extreme distaste for the follies and distractions of society, there was no corresponding inclination to turn to God. How truly attached to worldly things he must have been,

Jacqueline reflected, thus to resist the graces that God was sending him and to turn a deaf ear to His appeal!

They broke off to attend Vespers: Pascal under the small visitor's cupola, and Jacqueline behind the grill, praying as I am sure she had never prayed before, that the grace so visibly growing in her famous brother would lead him to take the last remaining step – into God's arms.

Some five weeks later, on the night of November 23, he took that step. Pascal's famous memorial to this experience, written in his own hand, was found sewn into his clothing at the time of his death. He had treasured it and had kept it on his person always. His sister Gilberte piously preserved it, crumpled and faded among his papers. It is a unique and intensely moving document which like some spiritual seismograph reflects in its very strokes and flourishes the fluctuations of his state of mind as he was writing it.

We may imagine him sitting at home in the evening. He opens his New Testament at the account of the Passion, and his eye fastens on Peter's thrice-repeated denial that he was an associate of Jesus. As he reads the cock crows – not for Peter, but for him, Pascal. Peter, confronted with his disloyalty, wept and so does Pascal, realizing that he too has separated himself from Christ.

What desolation, what darkness! Then suddenly deliverance comes, and he understands that he too can be forgiven; that he is forgiven.

He looks at his clock and sees it is half past ten. Seated at his desk, he begins his memorial. First, a tiny cross at the top of the paper, followed by the date – "Year of Grace 1654, Monday, 23 November, Feast of St. Clement, pope and martyr, and others belonging to the martyrology." Then the word "Fire," signifying "the God of Abraham, the God of Isaac, the God of Jacob," but not, he adds to rub in the point, "the God of the philosophers and scholars" – this, I am sure, with an eye on Descartes.

Now come the triumphant words: "Certainty, certainty, emotion, joy, peace, God of Jesus Christ. *Deum meum et Deum vestrum*, Thy God shall be my God. Oblivion of the world and of everything except God." His ecstasy is in his pen; the slanting letters proclaim it, like steeples reaching into the sky: "Joy, joy, joy, tears of joy!"

Now, like the saints Paul and Augustine in similar circumstances, Pascal had a craving for solitude, which he found at Port Royal's sister foundation, Port Royal des Champs.

Contrary to what is often suggested, the conversion that Pascal so ecstatically described in the memorial did not result in his abandoning all his worldly interests. For instance, he continued with his scientific studies and researches, and even as late as the last year of his life he was responsible for starting what was, in effect, the first public transportation system in Paris. Moreover, the most mundane of his writings, the famous *Lettres provinciales (Provincial Letters)* were undertaken, almost by chance, after his conversion and involved him as one of the principals in the bitter controversy then raging between the Jesuits and the Jansenists.

The Jesuits favored tempering the severities of Christian doctrine and practice in order to make them more palatable; the Jansenists were insistent that the service of Christ still required the renunciation of worldly pleasures and prizes. Pascal, in any case, would have been temperamentally on the Jansenist side. He loved the pleasures and the prizes much too much to tolerate any mitigation of their ill-repute. As it happened, Port Royal was in effect the headquarters of militant Jansenism, and his beloved Jacqueline one of the most ardent of the militants; he soon became their anonymous and enormously impressive spokesman.

Using to the full his splendid gift of irony, which he deployed in a lucid, flexible style more reminiscent of Jonathan Swift than Thomas Aquinas, Pascal mercilessly lambasted the Jesuits. It was a superb performance, greatly admired by the reading public, who flocked to get the letters as they came out. Despite – or perhaps because of – the letters' great popularity, some of the more staid Jansenists found them a shade disconcerting. The Jesuits of course abominated them.

The controversy which gave rise to the *Lettres provinciales* is the everlasting one between those who think that as far as possible we should be allowed to do what we like in this world, and those who, like Pascal, conceive it to be the glory and the greatness of man to look upwards from what he called "licking the earth," to survey the destiny that awaits him beyond the ticking of the clock. Today the controversy ranges round the concept of what is called situational ethics, whereby an act is right or wrong, not intrinsically, but in relation to its circumstances. As Pascal himself put it, nothing is just in itself merely according to reason; everything varies according to the weather. Now, as in Pascal's time, some individual Jesuits would agree.

Who won in the controversy between the Jesuits and the Jansenists? This is what everyone always wants to know; but of course, in truly fundamental disputes like the one between the Jesuits and the Jansenists, between the worldly and the other-worldly, there are no clear-cut winners and losers. It is perfectly true that Jansenism as such has ceased to exist. Persecution followed the appearance of the *Lettres provinciales*, and the religious at

Port Royal were required to adhere to an equivocal statement of orthodoxy – an exercise in casuistry that killed poor Jacqueline, or at any rate hastened her early death. Later, on the orders of Louis XIV, the Port Royal of Mère Angélique and the *gentlemen-hermits* was destroyed. As for the Society of Jesuits, they can be said to be going strong, or at any rate going.

Likewise, the Palace of Versailles, which Louis XIV took such pains to have built at the same time as he was destroying Port Royal, still stands – though it is no longer the residence of kings, but a tourist attraction. As for the *Lettres provinciales*, they hold their place in Pascal's *oeuvre*, but as literature (or perhaps better, as an early, brilliant essay in journalism) rather than as an apologia for Jansenism.

How then do the accounts work out? The answer is that they are still not closed, and never can be. Versailles, standing, is essentially as much a ruin as Port Royal ruined.

What Pascal defended cannot be lost. What the Jesuits still defend is lost already. They build the walls of Jericho – which have to be built, but only to fall whenever a Pascal blows his trumpet. While the Jesuits were concerned with tactics, Pascal's mind was on strategy.

In Pascal's time as in ours, the Church's continued existence was threatened from without and from within. The Reformation, like the discoveries and pretensions of science today, had challenged its basic premises, and inside the Church there were those – again, as there are today, in each case with the Jesuits well to the fore – eager to fall in with the new, trendy intellectual and moral attitudes.

Pascal was ready to use his dialectical skill in opposing the innovators, and considered himself to the end of his days a loyal son of the Church, even though he was open to a charge of heresy, and only just missed being excommunicated.

At the same time, what Pascal was concerned with essentially was not an institutional Church or a temporal State, but man himself: that fugitive from reality who must somehow be persuaded to confront his own imperfection and despair, and see through them into the bright light of eternity, his true habitat. "Since men are unable to cure death, misery, ignorance, they imagine they can find happiness by not thinking about such things." Well, Pascal would set them thinking.

Pascal was endlessly fascinated by the ingenuity with which we human beings evade reality. What an extraordinary thing it is, Pascal observed in the *Pensées*, that a man who has suffered some terrible bereavement or has become involved in some desperate plot can forget his troubles so easily. Born to know the universe, to sit in judgment and to rule, he is wholly concerned with trivialities. And if he tries to rise above them, he will only be departing from his natural state, neither angel nor beast, but just man.

Then there are the larger evasions of reality: for example, those mounted in courts of justice and of kings, on battlefields and in legislatures, in laboratories and universities. Thus Pascal anatomized our human condition in his great work, the *Pensées*.

> It is the nature of self-esteem and of the human self to love only oneself and to consider oneself alone. But what can a man do? He wants to be great and finds that he is small; he wants to be happy and finds that he is unhappy; he wants to be perfect and finds that he is riddled with imperfections; he wants to be the object of men's affection and esteem and sees that his faults deserve only their dislike and contempt. The embarrassing position in which he finds himself produces in him the most unjust and criminal passion that can possibly be imagined; he conceives a mortal hatred of the truth which brings him down to earth and convinces him of his faults. He would like to be able to annihilate it, and, not being able to destroy it in himself, he destroys it in the minds of other people. That is to say, he concentrates all his efforts on concealing his faults both from others and from himself, and cannot stand being made to see them or their being seen by other people.

In the high tide of his new-found faith, Pascal took upon himself the stupendous task of producing no less than a defense of the Christian religion. It was an audacious undertaking: to take, as it were, the contemporary atheist by the scruff of the neck and make him see how mistaken he was in rejecting what alone could save him from boredom and despair.

As things turned out, he never got beyond preparing the notes, and his sister Gilberte, in her charming memoir of him, bemoans the fact that all his labors should thus have been fruitless. She need not have worried. The notes, called *Pensées*, have enchanted, infuriated, uplifted, depressed, enlightened, mystified, but always enthralled countless readers from generation to generation and are today as sparkling as when they were written and, if anything, more relevant.

Indeed, I consider that it was a beneficent, if not miraculous, circumstance that Pascal was unable to proceed beyond the notes. The full work, had he lived to complete it, might well have been too massive, too definitive, too dogmatic even in its final conclusions, to appeal, as the *Pensées* have, to all the stragglers and vagrants, like myself, similarly questing. It might also have lacked something of the quality I find most delectable: a beautiful skepticism that contrasts joyously with the sentimentality and credulity of scientific humanism, which actually takes seriously man's ridiculous pretension to shape his own destiny, pursue his own happiness, and construct his own well-being.

"The red robes of our judges," Pascal insisted, "the ermine in which they swaddle themselves like furry cats, the courts where they sit, the *fleurs-de-lis*, all the august display is very necessary." Likewise, if physicians did not have cassocks and mules and professors did not have square hats and robes four sizes too large, they would never have been able to fool people. Kings and prelates and statesmen are under a similar necessity to dress up in their preposterous robes and gowns and decorations. Otherwise, we should see them for what they are: ham actors in an interminable soap opera called History, in which a mighty Roman Empire stands or falls on Cleopatra's nose, and whole continents are devastated by wars and revolutions purporting to uphold liberty and enlarge happiness, and inevitably destroying both.

Like a sublime kaleidoscope, Pascal presents us with thought after thought, all shining with truth as they come in mint condition from his brilliant mind:

> There is nothing which is so much in conformity with reason as the rejection of reason...
>
> Nature confounds the skeptics, and reason confounds the dogmatists. What, then, will become of you, O men, who seek to discover your true condition through your

natural reason? You cannot avoid one or the other of these sects, or live with any of them...

Jesus Christ did nothing but teach men that they only loved themselves; that they were slaves, blind, sick, unhappy and sinful; that he had come to deliver them, bring them light, sanctify and heal them; that this would come about through their hating themselves and following him to misery and death on the Cross...

We do not grow tired of eating and sleeping day after day, because hunger and fatigue return; without them, we should be bored. It would be the same without hunger for spiritual things; we should be bored. Hunger for justice is the eighth beatitude...

The heart has its reasons which are unknown to reason... It is the heart which is aware of God and not reason. That is what faith is: God perceived intuitively by the heart, not by reason...

What a vast distance there is between knowing God and loving Him...

Since your reason inclines you to believe and yet you cannot believe, your inability to believe comes from your passions. Try, then, not to convince yourself by multiplying the proofs of the existence of God, but by diminishing your passions...

When Plato and Aristotle wrote about politics, they were drawing up plans for a madhouse whose inmates – mankind – would be compelled to invent endless diversions to avoid confronting the circumstances of their existence, which would plunge them into despair, and to fight off the ennui which would otherwise afflict them.

"There is nothing so absurd that it has not been said by one philosopher or another," Pascal quoted Cicero as having said. The subsequent centuries have certainly not detracted from the force of this observation – least of all, our own.

To Pascal, what sort of creature was this monster man? "What a novelty, what a portent, what a chaos, what a mass of contradictions, what a prodigy! Judge of all things. A ridiculous earthworm who is nonetheless the repository of truth. A sink of uncertainty and error. The glory and the scum of the world. A chaos suspended over an abyss."

Man is great only in that he knows he is wretched. The very reason on which he so prides himself leads him to conclude that there are an infinite number of things beyond it. Pride separates him from God, and induces him to believe that he is a god himself. When he "licks the earth" he is cast into the other abyss and seeks his good in sensuality, which is the lot of the animals. Egomania and erotomania, the two sicknesses of the godless, afflict him.

In the *Pensées*, at the very moment of the birth of science as we know it today, Pascal prophesied its downfall – which we are witnessing. As men came to grasp the vast extent and complexity of creation, ranging between the minuteness of the atom and the immensity of the universe, they would become, as he predicted, terrified by the "eternal silence of these infinite spaces." A choice would confront them between seeing the whole future of man locked up immutably in his physical being, in his genes, or accepting with humility and contrition a role in the mysterious purposes of a loving God.

With passionate intensity, and with the clarity of an evening star shining in a darkening sky, Pascal plumped for the latter choice. If it was a wager, he would bet on it; if a vigil, he would watch for it; if a martyrdom, he would die for it. The alternative to God was nothingness. The way to God was revealed by Jesus Christ, who "is by His glory all that is great, being God, and is by His mortal life all that is stunted and abject. He assumed His wretched condition in order that He might be in all people and serve as a model for all conditions of men."

So Pascal takes us along with him on his own arduous mental and spiritual pilgrimage, delivering us at his destination, where we find the intersection of time and eternity in a Cross on which God dies in the person of a man, and a man rises from the dead in the person of God.

Pascal's funeral and burial took place in the church of Saint Etienne-du-Mont on August 21, 1662, at ten in the morning. Some fifty of his friends and relatives, including, of course, his sister Gilberte Perrier, gathered there for the ceremony. Pascal had expressed a wish to be buried in a common pauper's grave, so that he might lie near the poorest of the poor, who had become so very dear to him, and on whose behalf in the last year of his life he had sold all his possessions, keeping of all his books only the Bible and Saint Augustines's *Confessions* – a very wise choice. The Christian faith performs this miracle of humbling the greatest minds and proudest spirits – and when was there a greater mind or prouder spirit than Pascal's? – so that they may experience even before dying the joy of losing themselves in the great throng gathered round God's throne.

Later, controversies arose as to the attitude Pascal had to the Church on his deathbed, and about his mental and physical condition. I cannot myself see that either point was particularly material. We know that he ardently sought the consolations the Church has to offer to the dying, and that the eminent doctors who attended him more than lived up to the reputation for incompetence that Pascal's contemporary, the French writer Molière, was to give them in his comedies. Surely, this suffices. What Pascal bequeathed us as a permanent possession is, in Abbé Steinmann's words, the invaluable "inventory of the eternal problems" that he drew up. Also, his incomparable picture of man – ourselves – confronting an empty, silent and illimitable universe, in which the only choices before man are this emptiness and the crucified Christ. This being so, perhaps it is fitting that the only certain likeness we have of Pascal is his death mask.

william blake

1757 — 1827

We are all endlessly looking for reality even when we try not to, or think we are not. This applies particularly, of course, to poets, artists, mystics — even, in their own way, to philosophers and scientists. Though we pursue fantasy, never more so than today, the soul's only true sustenance is reality, which even in the most adverse circumstance it somehow finds, just as a seed falling on a rock face somehow finds the tiny crack where it can grow.

Of no English poet and artist is this more true than of William Blake. Born as the Renaissance world was coming to an end, he was profoundly distrustful of the intellect as a means of finding truth, and of science as a means of exploring it. Though he was the first, and perhaps the greatest, of the romantic poets, he lived to abominate the spirit of romanticism and all the license and disorder it involved.

I am wrapped in mortality, my flesh is a prison, my bones the bars of death. What is mortality but the things related to the body, which dies? What is immortality but the things related to the spirit, which lives eternally? What is the joy of heaven but improvement of the things of the spirit? What are the pains of hell but ignorance and bodily lust, idleness and devastation of the things of the spirit? The imagination is not a state, it is human existence itself.

It was this spiritual reality that Blake painted in his pictures and wrote about in his poetic compositions. He had no use for any other kind of reality, to the point that he could never bear to paint from what is called life, as expressed in flesh or substance or time, but only life's inward reality, or truth. The camera, representing the opposite principle, would have been anathema to him. Indeed, in my opinion, in a sense he prophesied its coming and pointed to its dangers when he wrote of how "We ever must believe a lie / When we see with, not through, the eye." His warning has passed unnoticed, but what a multitude and diversity of lies have, in consequence, come to be believed in!

I have no doubt myself that Blake was right, and that the only reality in life has been from the beginning of time, and will be till the end of time, a spiritual one called God. Blake's work is, to me, one of the great expressions of sanity that exist. Nor does it in the least surprise me that, for this very reason, he was in his time considered mad, and would today certainly be subjected to psychiatric treatment, with a view to drugging or psychoanalyzing and shocking him into what passes for sanity.

The faculty whereby Blake saw into the reality of things he called Imagination, and this is what he remained true to, from the beginning to the end, despite neglect, failure, penury, and other earthly ills that might well have deflected him from his central purpose.

> My mother groan'd, my father wept;
> Into the dangerous world I leapt,
> Helpless, naked, piping loud;
> Like a fiend hid in a cloud.

This was Blake's way of saying he was born. Actually, he was born on November 28, 1757, the third son of a London hosier, and christened William in the church of St. James, Piccadilly.

From the beginning, Blake was aware of Good and Evil as the two poles between which the current of life passes, generating the divine spark which exists in everyone.

> Every Night and every Morn
> Some to Misery are Born;
> Every Morn and every Night,

> Some are born to Sweet Delight;
> Some are born to Sweet Delight,
> Some are born to Endless Night.

Like the medieval artists, Blake personified Good and Evil as good and bad angels, not so much opposed to one another as complementary.

Blake instinctively rebelled against all forms of earthly authority, parental or ecclesiastical. Nonetheless, it was from the established Anglican Church that he derived much of his imagery, though for a time with the additional, somewhat eccentric influence of the Swedish theologian and mystic, Swedenborg, to whose teaching his parents adhered.

Blake's parents were in modest circumstance, and there would have been no possibility of his setting up as an artist, like, say, Sir Joshua Reynolds – one of his favorite butts. So he was apprenticed to an engraver, an excellent discipline for someone as ebulliently creative as Blake.

It gave him a life-long respect for fine drawing. As he put it himself in the light of his experience as an engraver:

> The great and golden rule of art, as well as of life, is this: that the more distinct, sharp and wiry the bounding line, the more perfect the work of art, and the less keen and sharp, the greater is the evidence of weak imitation, plagiarism and bungling. What is it that distinguishes honesty

from knavery, but the hard line of rectitude and certainty in the actions and intentions? Leave out this line and you leave out life itself; all is chaos again, and the line of the Almighty must be drawn out upon it before man or beast can exist.

By good fortune he was sent to copy figures in Westminster Abbey – a wonderful opportunity to develop his burgeoning genius at a time when there were none of the public galleries, collections and reproductions of the great masterpieces available to students today.

We can easily imagine the young Blake as a red-haired boy spending his days in the Abbey in blissful absorption. Breathing in history in the very air; seeing it all around him, written in monuments, some of which it was his business to study and to draw; sometimes, in his eagerness, climbing up on top of them so that he could look down, as well as up, at their gothic splendor. How incomparably more stimulating for him than helping his master, Basire, with other engravings! Basire, as a matter of fact, deserves a word of gratitude for having realized that with this particular apprentice, the only thing to do was to set him free with pencil and paper to follow his own fancies in the Abbey – a perfect place for this purpose.

Happily, the Abbey had not yet become a tourist shrine, a place to stare rather than to kneel. For the young Blake it was a place of worship, a house of God. Because of this he was never alone there, even when he was alone. Later in his life he was fond of recounting that while he was working in the Abbey he saw Christ and his Apostles at the altar, and a great procession of monks and priests, choristers and censer-bearers, and heard them chanting.

From these early days in the Abbey to the very end of his life, when he lay dying and burst out singing of the things he saw in Heaven, Blake was essentially, and in all matters, a *religious* man. I define this as meaning someone who, as Blake put it himself, has the capacity

> To see a World in a Grain of Sand
> And a Heaven in a Wild Flower,
> Hold Infinity in the palm of your hand
> And Eternity in an hour.

What is often overlooked nowadays is that Blake was also a Christian, even though he said and wrote things calculated to outrage and disconcert fellow Christians. For instance, priests and morality seemed to him the enemies, rather than the promoters, of true worship and virtue; and in Blake's notion of the marriage of Heaven and Hell, angels and devils are liable to change places, and a Jehovah-like God seems the enemy, rather than the

Father, of a beatific Jesus. Yet who has more beautifully stated the basic Christian need for the destruction of the ego, and the joy and liberation its subjection brings?

> He who binds to himself a joy
> Does the winged life destroy;
> But he who kisses the joy as it flies
> Lives in Eternity's sun rise.

Again and again, especially towards the end of his life, Blake saw in the Lamb of God the only true salvation for mankind, and in the subduing of fleshly passions, or rooting up the Infernal Grove, mankind's only true freedom. To see in this world the ultimate of Heaven, he insisted, was "the most Damnable Falsehood of Satan and his Antichrist." One of his somewhat mysterious poems, like so much of what he writes, to me seems to express perfectly the faith of this extraordinary man:

> Whate'er is Born of Mortal Birth
> Must be consumed with the Earth
> To rise from Generation free:
> Then what have I to do with thee?
>
> The Sexes sprung from Shame & Pride,
> Blow'd in the morn; in evening died;
> But Mercy chang'd Death into Sleep;
> The Sexes rose to work & weep.

Thou, Mother of my Mortal part,
With cruelty didst mould my Heart;
And with false self-deceiving tears
Didst bind my Nostrils, Eyes & Ears:

Didst close my Tongue in senseless clay,
And me to Mortal Life betray.
The Death of Jesus set me free:
Then what have I to do with thee?

Setting up on his own as an engraver in London, Blake
was not always able to choose his subjects but had to take
on such commissions as came his way – rather in the same
way that a free-lance commercial photographer must today. Thus we find him engraving advertisements, cartoons, the equivalent of travel brochures, and drawings
of social comment relating, for instance, to the explosive
subject of slavery. It was work he must often have found
distasteful, and he must have pined to live wholly in the
golden glory of his imagination. Even so, it enabled him
to make the acquaintance of many of his fellow artists,
some of whom became his lifelong friends.

One of the great blessings of his life was his marriage
to his wife Catherine, the daughter of a market gardener,
whom he met on the rebound from another courtship and
to whom he told his woes. Her sympathy was so lively
that he fell in love with her on the spot. She later recalled

that when she first set eyes on Blake, the conviction that this was the man she must marry so overwhelmed her that she nearly fainted. Her intuition proved correct.

It was just about two centuries ago that William Blake and Catherine Boucher were married in Battersea Parish Church. As was quite common at that time – and the way things are going it is likely to be quite common again – Catherine was illiterate, and so she signed her name in the register with a cross.

In the course of their long and happy marriage, Blake taught Catherine to read and write and also to draw, and she became a skilled engraver. From contemporary accounts and from Blake's own drawings of her, it appears that she was a woman of very considerable beauty, with large, dark eyes and a face with a great deal of character in it. They first set up house together in Green Street, in what is now Leicester Square. They were poor then and remained poor all their lives, so she had to be a very careful housewife.

If Blake in the course of his marriage went through moods in which he felt that marriage itself was a kind of bondage, it is only what has happened to everyone who has been married, whether wife or husband. What is absolutely certain is that their union grew deeper with the years, becoming an integral part of Blake's visions and sense of eternity.

As Blake came to see very clearly, and this is certainly my own view from experience, marriage is only possible in a continuing human relationship when it is directed in the first place towards the procreation of children, and finds in its ultimate fulfillment a spiritual union of which the bodily one is but a premonition. As the English poet John Donne put it:

> Love's mysteries in souls do grow
> And yet the body is His book.

Blake's marriage, as it happens, was not blessed with children; this must have been a sore disappointment to him, since, as his *Songs of Innocence* so enchantingly show, he understood children wonderfully and loved them dearly. Indeed, they crop up as themes throughout his work.

Catherine's love and devotion were wonderful and beautiful. According to Blake's biographer, Alexander Gilchrist, "she would get up in the night, when he was under his very fierce inspirations, which were as if they would have torn him asunder...sitting motionless and silent, to stay him mentally, without moving hand or foot; this for hours, and night after night."

Everyone who, like Blake, has a passion for goodness cannot but in some degree hate morality; just as lovers of freedom hate laws, and lovers of truth hate dogma.

There are many brilliant phrases and lines in Blake's writings in this sense. For instance:

> I went to the Garden of Love,
> And saw what I never had seen;
> A Chapel was built in the midst,
> Where I used to play on the green.
>
> And the gates of this Chapel were shut,
> And "Thou shalt not" writ over the door;
> So I turn'd to the Garden of Love
> That so many sweet flowers bore;
>
> And I saw it was filled with graves,
> And tomb-stones where flowers should be;
> And Priests in black gowns were walking their rounds,
> And binding with briars my joys & desires.

Or in "The Voice of the Devil" from *The Marriage of Heaven and Hell* – and remember it is the Devil who is speaking:

> Energy is the only life, and is from the Body...
>   Those who restrain desire, do so because theirs is weak enough to be restrained...

"The road of excess leads to the palace of wisdom," was another proverb of Hell.

On the strength of such observations as these Blake has been taken as a sort of patron saint of permissiveness.

Nothing could be more false. He saw as clearly as anyone who ever lived that to abandon himself to his sensual
appetites would be to cut himself off irretrievably from
his visions:

> Till I turn from Female Love,
> And root up the Infernal Grove,
> I shall never worthy be
> To step into Eternity.

The truth is that in our imperfect, mortal existence, morality is a condition of goodness, as law is of freedom, and
as dogma has been of the survival of our Christian faith.

London was Blake's world. How often, pacing its
streets, have I found his words echoing in my mind:

> I wander thro' each charter'd street,
> Near where the charter'd Thames does flow,
> And mark in every face I meet
> Marks of weakness, marks of woe.
>
> In every cry of every Man,
> In every Infant's cry of fear,
> In every voice, in every ban,
> The mind-forg'd manacles I hear.
>
> How the Chimney-sweeper's cry
> Every black'ning Church appalls;
> And the hapless Soldier's sigh
> Runs in blood down Palace walls.

But most thro' midnight streets I hear
How the youthful Harlot's curse
Blasts the new born Infant's tear,
And blights with plagues the Marriage hearse.

Though Blake belonged in time to the eighteenth century, he foresaw with remarkable prescience the industrial revolution that lay ahead, and how inimical it would prove to the life of the imagination that he so prized. Already in his lifetime the machine was destroying craftsmen, not just engravers like himself, but all who exercised such skills and crafts.

On the title page of Francis Bacon's *Essays*, Blake scribbled by way of comment: "Good advice for Satan's Kingdom." I like this very much. Heaven knows what he'd have written on other works in the same vein, like Darwin's *Origin of Species* and Huxley's *Science and Education*.

The notion of progress and the perfectibility of man, as expressed by Shelly's father-in-law, Godwin, had no more ferocious opponent than Blake, who rightly saw in it all the dreadful potentialities of human arrogance and destructiveness whose fulfillment we have witnessed in our time.

What some saw as the Enlightenment, Blake saw as a sort of a plague spreading over the Western World. He saw in Newton, the father of modern physics, the symbol of this coming age of human self-sufficiency, all of whose begetters were anathema to him:

> Mock on, Mock on Voltaire, Rousseau;
> Mock on, Mock on: 'tis all in vain!
> You throw the sand against the wind,
> And the wind blows it back again.

In the most widely known of Blake's poems (that is, the lines in the preface to his *Milton*, beginning: "And did those feet in ancient time / Walk upon England's mountains green?"), the phrase "dark Satanic Mills" is generally taken as referring to the abominations of the Industrial Revolution. As a result, the poem has become a sort of political hymn to be used at the more solemn, revivalistic Labor party occasions, such as the funeral of a leader, or the closing session of a party conference. Actually, of course, it was much more the Loom of Locke that Blake had in mind than any Lancashire mill. Blake's imagination told him that all evil things begin with lies and false teaching and lead to conflagration, conflict and despair. The feet that in his poem walked upon England's mountains green – the Countenance Divine that shone forth upon our clouded hills – did not belong to Karl Marx, but to the risen Christ.

With his imaginative insight, however, Blake also understood that the whole nature of man's productive process for meeting his needs was changing:

And all the Arts of Life they chang'd into the Arts
    of Death in Albion.
The hour-glass contemn'd because its simple
    workmanship
Was like the workmanship of the plowman,
    & the water wheel
That raises water into cisterns, broken & burn'd with fire
Because its workmanship was like the workmanship
    of the shepherd;
And in their stead, intricate wheels invented, wheel
    without wheel,
To perplex youth in their outgoings & to bind to
    labors in Albion
Of day & night the myriads of eternity: that they
    may grind
And polish brass & iron hour after hour, laborious task,
Kept ignorant of its use: that they might spend the
    days of wisdom
In sorrowful drudgery to obtain a scanty pittance
    of bread,
In ignorance to view a small portion & think that All,
And call it Demonstration, blind to all the simple
    rules of life.

So beginning with Bacon, a great transformation was taking place in the human condition. The machine, first seemingly a servant, would infallibly become a demonic master, poisoning our air, polluting our rivers and lakes, flattening our landscape, destroying our handicrafts and our art, and smothering the imagination whereby man's creativity could relate itself to God.

The two great upheavals of Blake's time, the American and French revolutions, were part of this same apocalyptic vision, and were treated accordingly. The putting down of tyrants, the freeing of slaves, the exposing of the moral Christian and his Laws – to all this Blake exuberantly responded; but then, he also saw that Caesar's poisoned crown would just adorn another brow:

> The hand of vengeance found the Bed
> To which the Purple Tyrant fled;
> The iron hand crushed the Tyrant's head
> And became a tyrant in his stead.

In the end Blake came to see that the only true freedom is spiritual, achieved through the imagination, and that the notion of progress in the world of space and time is an illusion that beguiles mankind with false hopes.

In his prophetic books – so difficult to understand and yet with a glowing core of meaning – he conveyed his sense of the doom that would befall men if they came to believe they could shape and dominate their own destiny. Their god, Urizen, was seen as drowning in the waters of materialism. Today, Blake, if he were in a position to observe the contemporary scene, would see western man likewise drowning in his own affluence.

For one short period of his life, Blake did move out of London and into the country, on the persuasion of his friend and patron William Haley, who provided him with a picturesque little cottage near the sea at Felpham in Sussex. In the long run the arrangement did not work and resulted in bitter reproaches and quarrels. Haley quite failed to appreciate the quality of Blake's work, and Blake found Haley's requirements a tedious servitude. It was during this period that Blake was arrested on a trumped-up charge of sedition. He was accused by a private in the dragoons of having said "Damn the King," and that he would help Napoleon Bonaparte if he came to England. This led to a trial of sedition on January 11, 1804. He was finally acquitted amidst, according to the *Sussex Advertiser*, "uproarious applause."

This experience preyed upon him to an abnormal degree and left its mark in his *Prophetic Books*. Even so, his sojourn at Felpham gave Blake some enchanted moments, reviving in him the mood of his exquisite *Songs of Innocence*.

Piping down the valleys wild,
Piping songs of pleasant glee,
On a cloud I saw a child,
And he laughing said to me:

"Pipe a song about a Lamb!"
So I piped with merry cheer.

"Piper, pipe that song again;"
So I piped: he wept to hear.

"Drop thy pipe, thy happy pipe;
Sing thy songs of happy cheer:"
So I sung the same again,
While he wept with joy to hear.

"Piper, sit thee down and write
In a book, that all may read,"
So he vanish'd from my sight,
And I pluck'd a hollow reed,

And I made a rural pen,
And I stain'd the water clear,
And I wrote my happy songs
Every child may joy to hear.

And:

> Little Lamb, who made thee?
> Dost thou know who made thee?
> Gave thee life, & bid thee feed
> By the stream & o'er the mead;
> Gave thee clothing of delight,
> Softest clothing, woolly, bright;
> Gave thee such a tender voice,
> Making all the vales rejoice?
> Little Lamb, who made thee?
> Dost thou know who made thee?

Little Lamb, I'll tell thee,
Little Lamb, I'll tell thee:
He is called by thy name,
For he calls himself a Lamb.
He is meek, & he is mild;
He became a little child.
I a child, & thou a lamb,
We are called by his name.
Little Lamb, God bless thee!
Little Lamb, God bless thee!

And:

The Sun does arise,
And make happy the skies;
The merry bells ring
To welcome the Spring;
The skylark and thrush,
The birds of the bush,
Sing louder around
To the bell's cheerful sound,
While our sports shall be seen
On the Echoing Green.

Old John, with white hair,
Does laugh away care,
Sitting under the oak,
Among the old folk,
They laugh at our play,
And soon they all say:

"Such, such were the joys
When we all, girls & boys,
In our youth time were seen
On the Echoing Green."

Such moments, like childhood itself, could not last. After innocence comes experience; the flowers and the fragrance give place to the "tiger's fearful symmetry," and nightmare figures lie in wait "in the forests of the night."

When the stars threw down their spears,
And water'd heaven with their tears,
Did he smile his work to see?
Did he who made the Lamb make thee?

Blake returned to London, more than ever feeling that he was an Ishmael, as he put it, born with a different face. Misfortunes, often brought on by his own odd disposition and whimsical ways, multiplied, and made him at times feel that he was the particular target of the world's buffetings. Yet he managed to avoid the self-pity to which his contemporary Rousseau was so given. Rather, Blake saw himself as Job, who would be the subject of one of his greatest masterpieces. Like Job, he accepted God's chastisement as something to be endured, something that would in the end purify and enlighten: "Though he slay me, yet will I trust in him."

So, ever cheerful, never lacking friends, Blake continued to the end, looking assiduously into the mystery of things, and providing thereby unique illumination for generations to come.

I must confess that when I first saw Blake's life mask, and that was quite a number of years ago, I was a little disappointed and surprised. It did not seem like the face of a poet and visionary. More like a man of action, I thought. As a matter of fact it by no means tallies with contemporary descriptions of Blake. For instance, one by the friend of his later years, Crabb Robinson, who said that at age sixty-eight "he had a large pale face, a full dark eye, a benignant expression – at the same time an air or languor except when he was excited, and then he seemed full of inspiration."

Even so, I think there is a lot to be learned about Blake from the life mask. The toughness and severity and tension it shows are the intimations of a life full of worldly hardships and disappointments, but elevated and illumined by the joy and lovingness and beauty which his eye of imagination saw all creation to be overflowing with:

> Joy and woe are woven fine,
> A clothing for the soul divine,
> Under every grief and pine
> Runs a joy with silken twine.

It is right it should be so;
Man was made for joy and woe;
And when this we rightly know,
Through the world we safely go.

So Blake expressed it. There are few lines I have said over to myself more often than these, always deriving comfort from them.

Blake's reputation for eccentricity, if not madness, was much promoted by the casual matter-of-fact way he spoke about his encounters with spirits from the past. Thus, he would say, as though it was the most natural thing in the world, that he had been chatting with Socrates or Milton. When Crabb Robinson asked him what language he talked with Voltaire, he answered: "To my sensations it was English. It was like the touch of a musical key; he touched it probably in French, but to my ear it became English." It was a shrewd answer. It is an illusion to suppose that those who look into eternity are simpletons when the children of time seek to trip them up. The Pharisees discovered this.

Quite often Blake made drawings of his spiritual visitors. These are the famous visionary heads, at which he would sometimes work all night long. Various of his friends have left accounts of him thus engaged; seated with his paints and looking intently at what appeared to the onlooker to be an invisible model. Once when he was working on William Wallace, he had to break off because, he said, Edward I "has stepped in between him and me." He thereupon polished off the King before returning to Wallace.

On another occasion, he told a visitor he had a great rarity to show him. This turned out to be "a naked figure with a strong body and short neck – with burning eyes which long for moisture, and a face worthy of a murderer, holding a bloody cup in its clawed hands, out of which it seems eager to drink." "But what in the world is it?" his visitor asked. "It is a ghost, sir," Blake replied. "The ghost of a flea – a spiritualization of the thing!"

Was all this, then, just hallucinations? Was Blake in this sense mad? There were some who thought so, while recognizing the high quality of his work – among them, men of letters like Wordsworth, Hazlitt and Lamb. Others, like the young friends and admirers who gathered round him at the end of his life, were convinced of his sanity. "Of all men whom I ever knew," a friend wrote, "he was the most practically sane, steady, frugal and industrious."

I personally incline to the latter view. In a materialist age like ours nothing is real except what is false. People believe in money, for instance, but not in God, whereas money is a fantasy, but God is the living truth. When the disciples saw Jesus after the Resurrection, his presence was more real to them than it had been during his lifetime – so real that they founded a religion on it which has lasted for two thousand years. Similarly with Blake's spiritual visitants. Even someone as spiritually obtuse as I am has seen in a face full of goodness a beauty far more dazzling and memorable than any in the flesh can show.

> Seek love in the Pity of other's Woe,
> In the gentle relief of another's care,
> In the darkness of night and winter's snow,
> In the naked and outcast. Seek Love there!

Mad? I should say sane to the point of sublimity.

Blake's worldly circumstances did not improve with the years. He grew poorer and poorer, and professionally speaking was almost totally forgotten. Crabb Robinson described the little bedroom he worked in, looking onto the river and just a few yards away from the noisy Strand, as "squalid and poverty stricken." Nonetheless, Blake received his friend there as though it had been a palace. Blake's wife Catherine, Robinson said, seemed to be the very woman to make him happy, "She had been formed by him...indeed otherwise she could not have lived with him."

Through these years of poverty and neglect Blake only grew more serene. No one need doubt his sincerity when he offered prayers of thankfulness to God that riches and fame had not come to him to blur, distort and obscure his vision. On the day of his death, August 12, 1827, some three months before his seventieth birthday, Blake lay in bed, a friend who was there recalled, singing songs so divinely, so beautifully, that Catherine got up to listen better, and then he turned to her and said, "They're not mine you know" and repeated it more emphatically, "They're not mine." Then he went on to tell her that they would never be parted, and that after he was dead, he would continue to watch over her just as he had during the years of their long companionship.

Blake had said before that to him death would be no more than moving from one room to another, and so it proved to be. He went on singing in his bed in the same divine way until about six in the evening, and then – as he said in one of his poems – silently, invisibly, the human spirit left him, becoming part of the eternity on which his eyes had been so faithfully set during his mortal years. A neighbor, a simple person who had come in to sit with Mrs. Blake, said that they had been present at the death not of a man "but of an angel," and I agree.

søren kierkegaard

1813 – 1855

The prophets, when they appear on our earthly scene, are rarely as expected. A king is awaited, and there is a birth in a manger. The venerable, the bearded, the portentous are usually spurious.

One of the oddest prophets ever was Søren Kierkegaard – a melancholic Dane, a kind of clipperty-clop, ribald Hamlet who from the middle of the last century peered quizzically into this one, dryly noting, before they happened, such tragicomic phenomena of our time as universal suffrage, mass media and affluence abounding.

Kierkegaard was insistent that the only way out of these gathering clouds of fantasy was to climb doggedly upwards to the rocky peak above them, where God dwells.

The greatest single influence on Søren Kierkegaard was undoubtedly that of his father, who was a harsh, dour, guilt-ridden man, deeply religious in his own way, and certainly a dutiful parent – yet somehow stricken. Søren was his youngest child and his favorite, and the intimacy between them was very great.

Then one day, some secret was disclosed. We do not know exactly what it was, but Søren wrote that the effect upon him was as though he had been in an earthquake. Thenceforth their intimacy was broken. An idol had been overturned, and Søren Kierkegaard stood among the broken pieces, needing to look for another father. This quest was to take him far beyond the narrow moral confines of his earthly father; far beyond the rigid creed and austere liturgy of the church. A quest more in keeping, perhaps, with the countryside of Jutland, with its wild storms and furious winds, but reaching beyond them, too – reaching beyond time itself, and into eternity.

Kierkegaard's father left Jutland as a boy to seek his fortune in Copenhagen, where he throve. Besides becoming very rich, he acquired the reputation as a man of wide reading and intellectual attainments. Nonetheless, there remained a cloud over his life. As a poor shepherd boy he had cursed God for the hardness and frustration of his life and had, in consequence, suffered ever after from a sense of having sinned. Another source of remorse was his seduction of a woman working in his house. Within a year of his first wife's death he married the other woman to legalize a daughter she bore him four months after their wedding.

Kierkegaard and his father were particularly intimate. The father watched over Søren's studies and tried to protect his son from the sins he was so morbidly conscious of having committed, especially those of the flesh.

Kierkegaard's mother, who appears to have remained almost a servant in the house, is ignored in all of his subsequent reminiscences about his childhood. When Kierkegaard, as a child, asked to be taken for a walk, his father would suggest that instead they remain inside and travel in their imagination. Thus, the two of them would walk together, pounding round and round the room. Some of the father's congenital melancholy undoubtedly infected and stayed with the son. In one of his stories Kierkegaard described a young boy turning over pictures of men the world considers to be heroes, among them the crucified Christ. Kierkegaard asked his readers to consider the effect of such an experience on a child. The effect on Kierkegaard, undoubtedly the boy in the story, was to make him question the nature of a world that could thus punish virtue and truth.

One of Kierkegaard's favorite places was Gilbjerg, a high spot whose view fascinated him.

From this spot I have seen the sea rippled by a soft breeze, seen it play with the pebbles. From here I have seen its surface transformed into a passive cloud of sea spray and heard the falsetto notes which come before the low bass of the storm. Here I have seen, so to speak, the emergence of the world and its destruction – a sight which truly calls for silence. I, of course, would rather not speak of those who see nothing bigger in nature than matter: people who really regard heaven as a cheese dish cover and men as maggots who live inside it.

In 1835, when he was twenty-two, Kierkegaard experienced one of the recurring crises in his life – a juncture he would have called an Either/Or situation. His theological studies, unlike his brother Peter's, were going badly and he was wasting time on other pursuits, some of them disreputable. There was always this gregarious, dissolute side of Kierkegaard's character to be considered: his love of company, a glass of wine, a pretty girl. The trouble, of course, arose in the other, the dark side, the seat of his angst, where the clouds of his congenital melancholy would gather.

His mood had been intensified by a whole series of deaths in the family: three of his sisters, then two of his brothers, and then his mother had died in rapid succession. As his brother Peter remarked, the survivors seemed to be spending all their time at the grave-side. It all appeared to confirm his father's conviction that a curse had been laid on him and his offspring. Like Faust his father had turned away from God, and the Devil had rewarded him by making him rich and respected. Now the time had come for the price to be paid, and Søren, as part of that price, was sure that he too would die young. How was he to shape up to so brief a sojourn here on this earth? Who was he supposed to be and what was he supposed to do?

"What I really need," he wrote at the time, "is to get clear what I must do, not what I must know. What matters is to find a purpose; to see what…really is God's will…that I shall do; the crucial thing is to find a truth which is truth for me."

This is what he was asking himself. How to establish contact with the reality he had already sensed in the universe, the quest for which made all others seem trivial and aimless? How to distinguish it from all the different sorts of fantasy – scientific, technical, political, erotic – which Western man was even then so busy constructing to evade this reality? How to get rid of all his own personal impediments – the ego lifting its cobra head, the appetites reaching out greedily like octopus tentacles? How to strip himself down until there was nothing, nothing at all, other than a sense of his own worthlessness? Perhaps at that point he might catch a fleeting glimpse of what he sought, and in catching that glimpse, find that there was a place for him after all in the great drama which Christ's life, death, and resurrection had unfolded to uplift, illuminate and redeem mankind.

In his writings (which he signed with more pseudonyms than almost any other writer) Kierkegaard recorded every thought and mood of his short life.

> We shall not be so arrogant as to do anything on a grand scale. Rather let us speak of a single individual human life and of the way it can be lived out here on earth. If one can see God in history, one can see him also in the life of the individual; to suppose otherwise is to delude oneself by yielding to the brutish imbecility which sees God only in the observations of nature; being taught, say, that Sirius is 180,000 million miles away from the earth. The materialistic man is astounded by such large data. If every single man is not an individual, simply by being human, then everything is lost and it is not worth hearing about great world-shaking historical events. But the world wants to be deceived.

Kierkegaard's first brush with the Danish establishment came not with the King (surprisingly enough, he and Christian VIII were on very friendly terms), nor with the Church (that was to come later), but with the Clown, in the person of a certain Goldschmidt, editor of a satirical magazine called the *Corsair*. Contrary to what is commonly supposed, the Clown is very much a part of the establishment *apparat* – as I discovered myself when I

was editor of *Punch*. There ought really to be a Clown
Laureate, as there is a Poet Laureate. As a matter of fact,
in practice, though not officially, there usually is one.
And it sometimes happens that the same person com-
bines the two roles.

Goldschmidt began by being a great admirer of Kierkegaard, and in fact described *Either/Or* as an "immortal
work." The two men had a slight acquaintance with one
another and met from time to time in the course of Kierkegaard's street ramblings. The cause of the row was a
man named Møller, an occasional clandestine contribu-
tor to the *Corsair*, whom Kierkegaard had known in his
student days as an attractive, amusing, wild young man.
Possibly he took him as the model for Johannes, the hero
of *The Seducer's Diary*, which was the nearest Kierkegaard came to writing an erotic book. In the course of an
article published in a literary review, Møller made some
disagreeable, personal remarks about Kierkegaard, who
much resented them and rather caddishly retaliated by
letting out that Møller contributed to the *Corsair* – a dis-
closure which prevented Møller from getting a Chair of
Aesthetics that he had set his heart on.

There the matter might well have rested; a typical episode in the notoriously backbiting literary circles in any
capital city. However, Kierkegaard felt bound to write to
Goldschmidt, in somewhat pompous terms, telling the

editor that he did not expect the friendly relations between them to protect him from being attacked by the
Corsair. Whereupon the magazine went to it with a will.
In cartoons, lampoons and satirical articles they ridiculed
Kierkegaard, especially his personal appearance – his
spindly legs, his trouser legs of different sizes, his large
nose, and the way he wore his hat down on his ears. They
parodied the intensity of his style and his many pseudonyms, made fun of his belief that he was a voice crying
in the wilderness, and even accused him of hypocrisy in
denouncing luxurious living when he himself was a rich
man and a lavish spender.

The attack was mounted so effectively and sustained
so long that it succeeded in making of poor Kierkegaard
a public figure of fun. Whenever he settled into his place
in church he was bound to hear someone muttering: "Ei-
ther/Or." He felt that all his peculiarities were under
constant scrutiny, including his trouser legs.

However much Kierkegaard may have disliked the
consequences, the row over the *Corsair* was deliberately
precipitated by him. Why? It seems to me that his spiritual development made him, by temperament, inclination and necessity, an outsider. Even an involvement like
marriage to a woman he undoubtedly loved, Regine, had
to be rejected. Even the money he inherited from his father, his only defense of his freedom and his privacy, was

to be spent as recklessly and speedily as possible, just to get rid of it.

Like all temperamental outsiders, Kierkegaard was given to roaming the streets, finding thereby anonymous companionship, and watching faces as they drifted by – intimates with whom there is no intimacy, beloved but requiring no words or touch of love, known and yet forever unknown.

One of the best descriptions of Kierkegaard is by a Scotsman named Hamilton, who, though they never met, observed him closely.

> There is a man whom it is impossible to omit in any account of Denmark, I mean Søren Kierkegaard. He is a philosophical Christian writer, evermore dwelling, one may almost say harping, on the theme of the human heart. There is no Danish writer more earnest than he, yet there is no one in whose way stand more things to prevent his becoming popular. He writes at times with an unearthly beauty, but too often with an exaggerated display of logic that disgusts the public.
>
> I have received the highest delight from some of his books. But no one of them could I read with pleasure all through.
>
> Kierkegaard's habits of life are singular enough to lend a, perhaps false, interest to his proceedings. He goes into no company, and sees nobody in his own house, which might as well be an invisible dwelling. I could never learn

that anyone had been inside of it. Yet his one great study is human nature. No one knows more people than he. The fact is he walks about town all day, and generally in some person's company.

Kierkegaard himself discussed his singularity and un-popularity.

> No doubt, what makes me unpopular is not so much the difficulty of my books as it is my personal life, the fact that even with all my endeavors I do not amount to anything, do not make money, do not get appointed to a job, do not become a Knight of Denmark, but in every way amount to nothing and on top of that am derided.

Kierkegaard was a kind of mystical schizophrenic. The two sides of his nature were at war, the imaginative and the polemical. In the latter capacity, like Swift, he was given to lacerating himself with furious indignation and getting involved in the intellectual, moral and even political controversies of his time.

In 1848, a time of great turmoil in Europe, two significant voices were raised, both, at the time, obscure and little heeded. One, Karl Marx's, proclaimed the ultimate and inevitable triumph of the proletariat in a world-wide class war, to be followed by the creation of a classless, socialist utopia, in which all government, all law, all exploitation of man by man, would wither away, and the human race live happily ever after.

The other voice, Kierkegaard's, scornfully dismissed such collectivist hopes for mankind as infallibly leading to a new and more comprehensive form of servitude. The divine right of kings had been abolished, but the divine right of the people which had replaced it would prove, Kierkegaard insisted, an even worse deception, and would give rise to regimes that exceeded any hitherto known in their brutality and claims to omniscience. I am the people – *Le peuple, c'est moi* – was an even more insanely arrogant claim than the famous one of Louis XIV's, *L'Etat, c'est moi* – I am the state.

No voice could have run more counter to the spirit of the age, the *Zeitgeist*, than Kierkegaard's. When freedom was seen in terms of counting heads, he spoke contemptuously of the fallacy of numbers, and of how, seen as a collectivity, human life must inevitably sink into a condition of brutishness and mindlessness. "When truth conquers with the help of 10,000 yelling men, even supposing that what is victorious is true, a far greater untruth is inculculated by virtue of the manner of their victory."

Against the new leviathan, whether in the guise of universal suffrage, democracy, or of an equally fraudulent triumphant proletariat, he pitted the individual human soul made in the image of a God who was concerned about the fate of every living creature. In contrast with the notion of salvation through power, he held out the hope of salvation through suffering. The Cross against the ballot box or the clenched fist; the solitary pilgrim against the slogan-shouting mob; the crucified Christ against the demagogue-dictators promising a kingdom of heaven on earth, whether achieved through endlessly expanding wealth and material well-being, or through the ever greater concentration of power and its ever more ruthless exercise.

Marx and Kierkegaard, the two key voices of the twentieth century. The curious thing is that though Marx purported to have an infallible scientific key to history, almost all his prophesies have failed to happen. On the other hand, Kierkegaard's forecasts, which were based purely on his imaginative intuition, have been fulfilled to a remarkable degree. Take, for instance, his profound sense that if men lost the solitude or separateness that an awareness of the presence of God alone can give, they would soon find themselves irretrievably part of a collectivity with only mass communications to shape their hopes, formulate their values and arrange their thinking.

> Suppose someone invented an instrument, a convenient little talking tube which, say, could be heard over the whole land...I wonder if the police would not forbid it, fearing that the whole country would become mentally deranged if it were used.

On the whole the evil in the daily press consists in its being calculated to make, if possible, the passing moment a thousand or ten thousand times more inflated and important than it really is. But all moral elevation consists first and foremost in being weaned from the momentary.

If Christianity is really to be proclaimed, it will become apparent that it is the daily press which will, if possible, make it impossible. There has never been a power so diametrically opposed to Christianity as the daily press. Day in and day out the daily press does nothing but delude men with the supreme axiom of this lie, that numbers are decisive. Christianity, on the other hand, is based on the thought that the truth lies in the single individual.

If someone adopts the opinion of the public today and tomorrow is hissed and booed, he is hissed and booed by the public. A nation, an assembly, a human being can change in such a way that they are seen to be no longer the same; but the public can become the very opposite and is still the same, the public.

It is very doubtful, then, that the age will be saved through the notion of social organization, of association. In our age the principle of association (which may at best have validity with respect only to material interests)…is an evasion, a dissipation, an illusion, whose dialectic is that as it strengthens individuals, so it weakens them. It strengthens by numbers, by solidarity, but from the ethical point of view this is a weakening. Not until the single individual has established an ethical stance in spite of the whole world, not until then can there be any question of genuinely uniting. Otherwise it gets to be a union of people who separately are weak; a union as unbeautiful and depraved as a child-marriage.

All this might seem a kind of hopelessness. But to Kierkegaard it alone offered hope. The acme of hopelessness would be to hope that so aimless, so unilluminated, so mindless a way of life as life without God could possibly work, or breed in those subjected to it anything but boredom and despair. In his words,

> The following changes will also occur. When the present generation, which has sought to level everyone and everything, to be emancipated, to revolt, and to demolish authority, has eliminated individualities and all that is organic and concrete, and has substituted such concepts as humanity and numerical equality among men, then individuals will be impelled to help themselves, each one individually. And then it will be said: "Look, everything is ready; look, the cruelty of these abstractions exposes the illusions of the finite; look, the abyss of the infinite is opening up; look, the sharp scythe of leveling permits all, every single individual, to leap over the blade; look, God is waiting! Leap, then, leap into the arms of God."

If that is being hopeless, may I never know hope! Kierkegaard also wrote:

> I once contemplated the possibility of not letting myself be taken over by Christianity, to do nothing else but expound

and interpret it, myself not a Christian in the final and most decisive sense of the word, yet leading others to Christianity.

And only now, with the help of heavy sufferings and the bitterness of repentance, have I perhaps learned enough about dying away from the world so that I can rightly speak of finding my whole life and my salvation through faith in the forgiveness of sins.

To those who caught a glimpse of him when, as often happened, he was meditating by himself in some lonely place, Kierkegaard must have seemed a bizarre little figure – a kind of comical monk. Or, better perhaps, a gargoyle looking down from the heights of his own audacious speculation at a world whose very imperfections and absurdities, by contrast, revealed God's presence and proclaimed his name.

Kierkegaard reflected much about reflection:

Reflection is in truth a benevolent helper which discovers and assists in finding where the absolute object of faith and worship is – namely, there where the difference between knowledge and ignorance collapses into a consciousness of ignorance, there where the resistance of an objective uncertainty tortures forth the passionate certainty of faith, there where the conflict of right and wrong collapses in absolute worship with absolute subjection. Reflection itself does not see the absolute, but it leads...the individual up to it, and says: "Here, I guarantee, when you worship here, you worship God."

When reflection is completely exhausted, then faith begins. Everything which reflection can hit upon, faith has already seen through and thought through and merged on the other side.

Those who see deeply into the nature of life are able to project this knowledge into the future, and so in some degree to foretell it. Thus we find Kierkegaard again and again diagnosing with uncanny precision the ills that would befall a materialistic society, especially when Christianity, the only possible corrective, partook of the same spirit – so that not only did science insist that men could live by bread alone, but the spirit of Christ was invoked to say that they should. Kierkegaard warned:

> In our time, the greatest menace comes from the natural sciences. Psychology will ultimately encompass ethics. And already there are intimations of a tendency to treat ethics as a brand of physics to be calculated statistically, working over averages as in calculating vibrations in laws of nature.

Foreseeing the obsessive interest to come in a social morality only vaguely related to personal behavior, Kierkegaard said,

> We have totally abolished the notion of imitation and at best hold to the paltriness called social morality. In this way men cannot become truly humbled so that they genuinely

feel the need of Grace. What is required of them is no more than social morality, which they fulfill tolerably well.

Is not the truth of the matter really this, that man is just like a child who would rather be free from being under his parents' eyes? Is not this what men want? To be free from being under the eyes of God? When Christ resolves to become the Savior of the world, a lament goes through all humanity. Sighing grievously they ask: Why do you do this? You will make us all unhappy. Simply because to become a Christian is the greatest human suffering. Christ, being an absolute, explodes all the relativity whereby we humans live. In order to live in the spirit rather than the flesh, as he requires, one must go through crisis after crisis, being made thereby, from a human point of view, as unhappy as it is possible to be.

As Kierkegaard became increasingly gripped by the great drama of the Christian faith, in his own terms moving into the third, or religious phase of his spiritual pilgrimage, it was almost inevitable that he should fall out with the Church. This nearly always happens, as a Wesley could find no place for himself in the Anglican establishment a century earlier, and a Tolstoy was to discover when he was excommunicated by the Russian Orthodox Church.

It would be hard to detect a saint in a temperament as cantankerous as Kierkegaard's; even his undoubted mystical insights were often laced heavily with irony. Yet without any question, as his short life drew towards its close, his sights were fixed ever more firmly on what is transcendental and eternal in our mortal life. It was for this reason that the Danish Church was particularly abhorrent to him – such a genial, worldly church, even the salaries of its clergy and bishops were paid for by the secular state. Nor is it in any way surprising that his venom was concentrated on the person of the celebrated, mundane Bishop Mynster, gifted and socially sought after, and his father's honored and respected spiritual adviser.

No doubt out of filial piety, Kierkegaard held his fire till Bishop Mynster died in January of 1854 and H. L. Martensen, his old theology tutor, had been appointed as the new bishop. Martensen had enraged him by referring to Mynster, in a funeral oration, as one of "the whole line of witnesses to the truth which, like a holy chain, stretched...through the ages from the days of the Apostles." If I apply this observation to any of the holders of the Sees of Canterbury and York during my lifetime, I have no difficulty whatsoever in understanding Kierkegaard's indignation.

Anyway, the first article was followed by ten others in the same strain, and the series was subsequently continued in some pamphlets he wrote called *The Instant*.

In essence, Kierkegaard was making exactly the same point as Pascal in the *Lettres provinciales*, which, incidentally, he had read about this time with great delight. Each one was insisting, in a different idiom and in quite different social circumstances, with all the irony and emphasis at his command, that the one sure way to abolish Christ's Kingdom, irretrievably and forever, was to make it "of this world." Pascal's shots were fired at the hair-splitting Jesuits, Kierkegaard's at the Danish clergy, which he insisted should, at all costs, be shunned:

> Parsons live by presenting the sufferings of others, and that is regarded as religion, uncommonly deep religion even, for the religion of the congregation is nothing but hearing this presented. As a religion…just about as genuine as tea made from a bit of paper which once lay in a drawer beside another bit of paper which had once been used to wrap up a few dried tea leaves from which tea had already been made three times.

Kierkegaard's scorn for church dignitaries applied equally to evangelistic social reformers. Here, too, Kierkegaard proved to be an uncannily accurate prophet. A century later we find churches of all denominations preoccupied with what is called the social gospel and often falling over one another as they struggle to get onto the revolutionary band-wagon – even though it is moving at top speed away from Golgotha and into the kingdoms of the earth that Christ so contemptuously rejected when the Devil offered them to Him. It was in making this prophetic and profoundly important point that Kierkegaard felt able, at last, to put aside all pseudonyms and mystifications and write as himself, facing whatever consequences might ensue.

Kierkegaard's words were little noticed outside Copenhagen, and even there soon forgotten, but they have proved to be uncannily prescient, to the point that everywhere today people are asking themselves whether perhaps this weird little Dane with the many pseudonyms might not, after all, have had the heart of the matter in him. He had hoped

> Through my writings...to leave behind me so accurate an account of Christianity in the world that an enthusiastic, high-minded young person will be able to find in them, as it were, a map of Christian relationships. I've not had any assistance in this form...the early Church Fathers whom I found failed in one essential qualification...they did not know the world.

Kierkegaard modestly called himself a Christian auditor – "An apostle proclaims the truth, an auditor is responsible for discovering counterfeits" – and therefore has to have been in his time a bit of a counterfeiter himself. Kierkegaard, however, achieved much more than just being an auditor or topographer of Christianity, he also charted a new course for others to follow: three stages, from the aesthetic, to the ethical, to the religious. He went through each of the stages himself, as he recounted in his books. In them, he was writing his own spiritual autobiography, which was why he used pseudonyms, each of which, even Johannes the seducer, represented some self he had explored and shed.

The aesthetic stage was the equivalent of paganism, seeking satisfaction through the senses, physical beauty, erotic excitement; satisfaction through the exercise of artistic skills, celebrity or riches, or success in any of its guises.

As for the ethical stage, it represented an awareness of God, though not an awareness of man's limitations. But what could be more ridiculous than man supposing he could make laws which were just, achieve brotherliness by means of an equitable distribution of wealth and opportunity, sustain a religious faith with only earthly ends, in short establish a Kingdom of Heaven on earth, with the clock ticking away eternity and elected parliaments exercising divine authority.

So he found himself relentlessly pushed into the third stage, the religious stage. This is where all the pseudonyms were put aside, and he became just Søren Kierkegaard, a poor sinner who knew nothing except that he existed now, with time as an eternal present, and that whatever fate might lie in store for mankind, they would never see in this earth their only habitat, or in history their only destiny.

In the aesthetic phase, life is an experience; in the ethical one, a process; but in the religious phase it is a drama – for Kierkegaard, an existential drama, in that its central character, the crucified Christ, exists now, thereby making now always.

A quality which I particularly admire in Kierkegaard is his courage, the courage of a man by nature timid and even cowardly. Having decided that his life must be dedicated to looking for reality, or God, he pursued this aim undeviatingly to the end, in spite of physical frailty and ill health, ridicule, loneliness, every sort of discouragement. His chosen mode of expression was the written word; a whole stream of books, articles, every sort of prose composition came from his pen. In the case of his books, he used up his inheritance to pay for their publication, so that on the day of his death, not one penny remained. His life and his money expired together.

By his forty-third year, Kierkegaard's life was exhausted, and in November of 1855 he died. His nephew thus described his end:

> Never have I seen the spirit break through the earthly husk and impart to it a glory as of the Transfigured Body on the resurrection morning.

He took my hand in both of his – how small they were and thin and palely transparent – and said only, "Thanks for coming, and now farewell," but these simple words were accompanied by a look the match of which I have never seen. It shone out from a sublime and blessed splendor which seemed to me to make the whole world light. Everything was concentrated in those eyes as the source of light, heartfelt love, blissful dissolution of sadness, penetrating clearness of mind, and a jesting smile.

These were some of Kierkegaard's last written words, expressing very beautifully the mood in which he died:

I have nothing more to add. But let me merely say this, which in a way is my life, is to me the content of my life, its fullness, its bliss, its peace and satisfaction. Let me express this, a view of life which comprehends the idea of humanity and of human equality: Christianity implies, unconditionally, that every man, every single individual, is equally close to God...How close and equally close? Because Loved by Him. Consequently there is equality, the equality of infinity, between man and man. If there is any distinction, it is that one person bears in mind that he is loved, perhaps day after day, perhaps day after day for seventy years, perhaps with only one longing, a longing for eternity so that he really can grasp this thought and go through life with it, concerning himself with the blessed occupation of meditating on how he is loved – and not, alas, because of his virtue. Another person perhaps does not remember that he is loved, perhaps goes on year after year, day after day, and does not think of his being loved; or perhaps he is glad and grateful to be loved by his wife, by his children, by his friends, by his contemporaries, but he does not think of his being loved by God. Or perhaps he laments not being loved by anyone and does not think of being loved by God. Infinite, divine love; it makes no distinction! But what of human ingratitude? If there is an equality among us men in which we completely resemble each other, it is that not one of us truly thinks about being loved!

fyodor dostoevsky

1821 – 1881

When the Bolsheviks seized power in Russia in the October Revolution of 1917, one of the first administrative
acts of the new revolutionary government was to transfer the capital from St. Petersburg, whose spirit, like its
elegant architecture, belonged to Western Europe, to
Moscow, at the heart of Russia and of Russian history.
At the time there was every reason – strategic, economic
and political – for doing this, but it also settled a controversy that had agitated and divided the Russian intelligentsia for years past – between the Westernizers and
the Slavophiles. Though the triumphant Bolsheviks
looked to a German Jew, Karl Marx, for their ideology,
and to the Twentieth Century's most successful expo-
nent of capitalism, America, for their technology, their
regime was to be, in its aspirations, its strategy and its
character, essentially and insistently Russian.

In October 1821, a second child was born to the resident doctor of a Moscow hospital then known as the Mariinskaya Hospital for the Poor. The baby who thus came into the world in an obscure enough way was destined to become one of the most famous writers of his time, not just in Russia but throughout the world. The doctor's name was Dostoevsky, and he christened his new son Fyodor.

Like so many of my generation, I first read Dostoevsky's novel, *Crime and Punishment*, when I was very young. I read it like a thriller, with mounting excitement. Later, when I came to read Dostoevsky's other works, especially his great masterpiece, *The Brothers Karamazov*, I realized that he was not just a writer with a superlative gift for storytelling, but that he had a special insight into what life is about, and into man's relationship with his Creator, making him a prophetic voice looking into and illumining the future. I came to see that the essential theme of all his writing is Good and Evil, the two points around which the drama of our mortal existence is enacted.

The Dostoevsky family's own circumstances were decidedly somber. His father seems to have had a harsh and irascible temperament, made worse by a growing tendency to drink too much; and his mother, naturally a cheerful soul, succumbed to tuberculosis during her ninth pregnancy, when Fyodor was fifteen. It was the end of family life for Dostoevsky; along with his brother Michael, he was sent off to St. Petersburg to prepare for early entry into the Military Engineering College there.

When Dostoevsky had been only some six months at the Engineering Academy, he heard that his father had died, allegedly murdered by some serfs on his estate in revenge for his admittedly drunken, incalculable and lecherous ways. For obvious reasons the family kept the details to themselves – even assuming they knew them with any certitude; the authorities, too, were anxious that such murders – apparently rather common at the time – should not be widely publicized. The death of his father, in circumstances so mysterious and so sinister, cannot but have affected Dostoevsky profoundly. It has even been suggested that it brought on the epileptic fits that were to afflict him for the rest of his life.

Dostoevsky's six years at the Engineering Academy seem to have left little mark upon him. In 1844, when he was twenty-three, he took the plunge, resigned his commission and set up as a writer in St. Petersburg – a hazardous enterprise, but almost immediately successful. *Poor Folk*, his first published work, a study in the Gogol-Dickens style of the poor of St. Petersburg, was rapturously received by, among others, Belinsky, the famous critic in whom Dostoevsky was later to see a misguided

Westernizer. Few writers have gotten off to so promising a start; everything seemed to be set fair for a dazzling career.

The Belinsky circle, like the Bloomsbury one and all such circles, was no doubt a great bore, and Dostoevsky found more exciting (and, as it turned out, dangerous) company in the Petrashevsky circle. This was a group of revolutionaries, all bent on overthrowing the existing social order. Inevitably, the Petrashevsky-ites were infiltrated by the secret police, and some thirty-four of them – Dostoevsky among them – were arrested and sent off for examination. He, like Shatov in *The Devils*, had been entrusted with the clandestine printing press.

Dostoevsky found himself in solitary confinement in the Peter and Paul Fortress where so many revolutionaries – Bakunin, for instance – were at one time or another incarcerated. For Dostoevsky it was the true beginning of his inner life, and of the illumination out of which his great works were to come. Prisons, let it be said, have fostered far more art and mystical insight than any Arts Council, Ministry of Culture or other such effort in the way of governmental encouragement. In the Peter and Paul Fortress he was willy-nilly introduced to the theme of punishment, which he was suffering, and crime, to which a long, elaborate examination sought to relate it. The punishment was tangible, the crime more elusive; in the questions put to him by his interrogator there is the same insistent repetition, the same cat-and-mouse tactics taking advantage of Dostoevsky's ignorance of the extent of his questioner's knowledge, as in the interrogation of Raskolnikov by Porfiry in *Crime and Punishment*.

Dostoevsky had been eight months in the Peter and Paul Fortress when the verdict was at last announced. Twenty-three of the prisoners, including Dostoevsky, were condemned to death, with a secret proviso by the Czar that in view of their youth, at the very last moment, the sentence should be commuted to a more lenient one. So the twenty-three condemned men were taken before an execution squad. The guns were actually lifted, the order to shoot was actually given, when one of the Czar's aides-de-camp rode dramatically up and announced a reprieve. In *The Idiot*, Prince Myshkin, on his first visit to the Yepanchins, describes a similar experience as happening to a friend of his:

> Three posts were dug into the ground about twenty paces from the scaffold, which was surrounded by a crowd of people and soldiers, for there were several criminals. The first three were led to the posts and tied to them; the death vestments (long white smocks) were put on them, and white caps were drawn over their eyes so that they shouldn't see the rifles; next a company of soldiers was drawn up

against each post…The priest went to each of them with the cross. It seemed to my friend that he had only five more minutes to live. He told me that those five minutes were like an eternity to him; riches beyond the dreams of avarice; he calculated the exact time he needed to take leave of his comrades, and decided that he could do that in two minutes, then he would spend another two minutes in thinking of himself for the last time, and, finally, one minute for a last look around…There was a church not far off, its gilt roof shining in the bright sunshine. He remembered staring with awful intensity at that roof and the sunbeams flashing from it; he could not tear his eyes off those rays of light; those rays seemed to him to be his new nature, and he felt that in three minutes he would somehow merge with them. The uncertainty and the feeling of disgust with that new thing which was bound to come any minute was dreadful; but he said that the thing that was most horrible to him was the constant thought: "What if I had not to die! What if I could return to life – oh, what an eternity! And all that would be mine! I should turn every minute into an age, I should lose nothing, I should count every minute separately and waste none!" He said that this reflection finally filled him with such bitterness that he prayed to be shot as quickly as possible.

Dostoevsky's sentence was "four years penal servitude, to be served in fortresses and then as a common soldier." At midnight he was fitted with ten-pound irons on his feet, and then taken in an open sledge to Siberia.

The four years he spent in the Omsk penal settlement, fettered and in the harshest conditions of confinement imaginable, were seemingly lost years; he wrote nothing and suffered much. Yet it might be doubted whether, without them, he would ever have been more than a gifted writer and man of his time. His own subsequent account, in *The House of the Dead*, is no more than the bare bones of the experience; the great works that follow probe and expound it. In *Crime and Punishment*, Raskolnikov is similarly sent to Siberia and, like Dostoevsky, begins by being proud and aloof with his fellow prisoners. Then he comes to see that they are brothers, too — "Many of them have profound, strong, beautiful natures... Some you cannot help respecting, others are downright beautiful." He makes Raskolnikov emerge from the terrible squalor and monotony and cruelty of prison life with a conviction that the experience of living is somehow more than dialectics.

Military service was a decided improvement — for instance, Dostoevsky could get letters and books, and an element of excitement was added by a frenzied love affair with a lady — Maria Dmitrievna Isaeva — who, after many turbulent meetings and partings, at last became his wife.

It took five years of maneuvering of one sort or another for Dostoevsky to be released from military service and get permission to return to St. Petersburg.

Finally he arrived there in December 1859, almost exactly ten years since he left in that open sleigh for Omsk. At first he occupied himself largely with journalistic work in collaboration with his brother Michael, overjoyed to be back in the swim, to have newspapers to read and polemics to engage in and friends to see. When, three months after the death of his wife, Maria, Dostoevsky's brother Michael died suddenly, he was left with financial responsibility for the magazine, *Epokha*, they had been jointly running. This involved him in chronic insolvency for years to come, but induced him to return to his true work, the first fruit being the appearance in 1866 of *Crime and Punishment* in serial publication.

The scene had to be St. Petersburg, one of those seedy neighborhoods where his long perambulations often took him – tall, shabby apartment blocks teeming with people coming and going, dark doorways and stairways. As for the crime, he was an avid reader of crime reports and found in the newspapers one that would suit perfectly. An aged moneylender, widow of a titular councilor, an old crone who lent grudgingly and collected avidly, had, along with her sister, been struck down with an axe in her own apartment. Times were hard, and there were many such moneylenders-cum-pawnbrokers in the district. Under the circumstances a certain amount of sympathy for her assailant might be expected.

He was Raskolnikov, one of Dostoevsky's great creations; his Candide (he had long projected a Russian nineteenth-century version), or perhaps his Faust or his Rastignac; an aspiring Hero of His Time as characteristic as Lermontov's; a down-in-the-mouth student who never studied; slothful and penniless, a half-baked intellectual with all the fashionable, current ideologies rattling about in his mind, moody and vain and given to violence in thought if not in word and deed.

At no point does Raskolnikov feel or express any pity for the murdered women, or remorse at having killed them. Nor does he seek to justify having murdered them by his need for money. In fact, he doesn't so much as look over his booty, but just hides it away on a building site where he can recover it if ever he has a mind to. In the days after the murder that he spends brooding on it, he experiences no regrets and knows no penitence; only fear, not so much that he will be found out, as that he will weaken and confess.

As it turns out, there is no occasion for him to confess. He is in the clear as far as the police are concerned, and yet he does confess – to Sonia, a pathetic girl who has taken to prostitution to help support the indigent household of her drunken father. He had come to realize, he tells her, that power is given only to him who dares to stoop and take it – "That's why I killed the old woman."

His only regret now is, he almost whimpers, that he has proved unequal to this high endeavor; he has come to Sonia to ask what he ought to do.

In the character of Raskolnikov, Dostoevsky takes us to the very ultimate in human godlessness, to the point at which man worships his own will and thereby finds his only sanctification in its exercise – ultimately in violence for violence's own sake. Violence in art and in literature and in entertainment, violence in thought and in deed, violence on the streets and on campuses, violence in football stadiums and in the cinema and on the television screen, violence in politics and in ideologies and even in religion. "I kill, therefore I am!" says Raskolnikov, and even as he says it he realizes that it was not the old hag he murdered, but himself. "I did myself in at one blow and for good," he tells Sonia. So it will be, Dostoevsky says to us, for all who follow this devil's way, whether singly or collectively.

It is in Sonia's mouth that Dostoevsky puts the answer:

"Get up!" She seized him by the shoulder and he raised himself, looking at her almost in astonishment. "Go at once, this very minute, and stand at the crossroad, bow down, first kiss the earth which you have defiled – and say to all men aloud: 'I am a murderer!' Then God will send you life again. Accept suffering and be redeemed by it – that's what you must do."

At first he rejects it, but at last, after his trial and forced exile to Siberia, where Sonia follows him, he sees in her love and devotion the possibility of a rebirth – of a gradual regeneration, of becoming acquainted with a new and hitherto unknown reality. Accept suffering and be redeemed by it – this was Dostoevsky's message to a world hurrying frenziedly in the opposite direction, seeking to abolish suffering and find happiness. Since Dostoevsky's time, the world has known much trouble and found little happiness, and so may be the better disposed to heed his words.

The severe financial difficulties in which his brother Michael's death involved Dostoevsky got him into the habit of retreating abroad when the pressure of his creditors became insupportable. This resulted in frequent stays at German spas – such as Wiesbaden – where a casino was provided to relieve the tedium of imbibing large quantities of distasteful medicinal waters. One wonders what the blameless bourgeois dyspeptics going to and from the *Kurhaus*, or listening to the orchestra in the gardens, made of the crazed-looking bearded Russian who had come among them.

In his short, brilliant novel, *The Gambler*, Wiesbaden and the other spas appear as Roulettenburg, and the hero, Alexis Ivanovich, is drawn as irresistibly to the tables as

Dostoevsky was. It was not, however, as Alexis Ivano-vitch explains, just the play's excitement; he wanted the money, wanted it desperately, and wanted it to come to him in this particular way – by sheer chance rather than by work or stratagem or calculation. How strange it is to think of this inspired writer sitting hour after hour, evening after evening, utterly absorbed in the monotonous repetition of *faites vos jeux, rien ne va plus,* with the players frenziedly staking their money, at the very last moment changing their minds and pulling some back or piling some more on; then the announcement of the inexorable number at which the little ball has come to rest, and the agonized calculations of winnings and losses.

Dostoevsky said of himself that he carried everything to excess – love and hate, hope and despair, ecstasy and sentimentality; gambling was, for him, the *reductio ad absurdum* of money. Just to get it and lose it on the turn of a wheel! To acquire riches by chance, and then lose them as suddenly and unaccountably! The banker, the speculator, even the prospector for gold might persuade himself that his cupidity performed some useful service, but gamblers are the monks of greed, dedicated wholly to its service, with the green baize tables for an altar on which to set out the sacrificial offerings of coins and banknotes. As money loses its value, will the cult go on? It is a possibility that Dostoevsky would have enjoyed exploring.

Some of Dostoevsky's most frenetic gambling excesses were associated with the most physical of his love affairs – with Apollinaria Suslova, a student who approached Dostoevsky initially in a mood of awe at his greatness, and then found him (a common campus drama) disappointing in bed. She appears in *The Gambler* as a willful *femme fatale*.

Writing *The Gambler* proved in every sense therapeutic. For financial reasons it had to be completed in twenty-six days, and to achieve this Dostoevsky procured the services of a stenographer, Anna Grigoryevna Snitkina, who turned out to be exceptionally competent and sensible, and in due course became his second and last wife. On their travels in Europe she had to endure one final gambling debauch, and writes in her diary the appalling straits to which it reduced them – the pawning of everything they had, including her wedding ring, at times the actual starvation to which they were subjected, all made worse for Anna because she was going through her first pregnancy. Then, again at Wiesbaden, the mania spent itself as mysteriously as it had begun, and for the last decade of his life, thanks to Anna's quiet competence, steady affection and careful management, Dostoevsky had the peace of mind to produce his great works in relative ease and security.

Dostoevsky, who normally stayed as far away as possible from museums and art galleries, paid a special visit to the Museum of Art in Basel to see a painting, "Christ Taken Down from the Cross," by Hans Holbein the Younger. He had heard about this picture, and what he had heard had greatly impressed him. His wife Anna described in her diary Dostoevsky's reaction to seeing the original:

> The painting overwhelmed Fyodor Mikhailovich, and he stopped in front of it as if stricken…On his agitated face was the sort of frightened expression I had often noted during the first moments of an epileptic seizure. I quietly took my husband's arm, led him to another room and made him sit down on a bench, expecting him to have a seizure any minute. Fortunately, it didn't come. Little by little Fyodor Mikhailovitch calmed down, and when we were leaving he insisted on going to take another look at the painting that had made such an impression on him.

Anna's own reaction was one of revulsion. She writes of the painting that, contrary to tradition, Christ is depicted "with an emaciated body, the bones and ribs showing, the hands and feet pierced by wounds, swollen and very blue, as in a corpse that is beginning to rot. The face is agonized, and the eyes are half open, but unseeing and expressionless. The nose, mouth and chin have turned blue." In *The Brothers Karamazov*, when the saintly Father Zossima dies, the monks are deeply disturbed because the body soon begins to stink, when, as a potential saint, it should have remained intact. This superstition was exposed in the early days of the Soviet regime in the anti-God museums — for instance, in the one set up in the ornate St. Basil's Cathedral in Red Square — by showing the fossilized remains of buried saints dug out of their graves. How ironic that opposite St. Basil's was the mausoleum in which the carefully preserved body of Lenin was on display, thus promoting a revival of the selfsame superstition the anti-God museums were supposed to have abolished.

The reason Anna was so horrified was that Holbein's picture shows the body of Christ in a state of decomposition. On the other hand, as far as Dostoevsky was concerned, the picture's fascination was precisely that it *did* show Christ's body decomposing. If His body was not subject to decay like other bodies, then the sacrifice on the Cross was quite meaningless; Christ had to be a man like other men in order to die for men. In other words, at the Incarnation, God did truly become a man.

Dostoevsky's wanderings outside Russia brought him, in 1867, to Geneva, where so many wanderers of one sort or another have come. On the shores of Lake Geneva, it is safe to say, more explosive words have been uttered and more explosive ideas entertained than anywhere else in modern times; from Rousseau to Lenin, it has been the seed-bed of revolution. As though to redress the imbalance, the city itself has remained one of the bastions of bourgeois orthodoxy when so many of its citadels elsewhere have been falling. An ideological adventurer may still deposit his savings in Geneva with a reasonable assurance that they will remain intact, whatever the consequences of the propagation of his ideas elsewhere.

Harassed by his usual money troubles and over the late delivery of his work – in this case *The Idiot*, which he was struggling to finish – Dostoevsky took a sour view of both the revolutionary ideas and their bourgeois cushioning. In his letters he complains equally of the awfulness of life in Geneva, on Sundays particularly, and of the various *enragés* assembled for an international congress under the auspices of a League for Peace and Freedom, some of whom – Herzen and Bakunin, for instance – were known to him. How many such congresses there were to be in Geneva, culminating in the largest, longest, most publicized and most futile, the League of Nations, whose fine new *Palais des Nations* was completed just when the organization itself, to all intents and purposes, had become an irrelevance.

For the title of his next novel, written in Geneva, Dostoevsky chose *The Devils;* * his theme is that, just as the devils entered into the Gadarene swine, the subversive ideas of the age were entering into people's minds and would similarly destroy them. Raskolnikov's insistence that he had a right to kill, translated into politics, led straight to Bakunin's dictum that destruction is in itself creative, and so to revolution for revolution's own sake. Thus, today's Raskolnikov is tomorrow's Nechaev – the young student revolutionary terrorist on whom Dostoevsky based the character, Pyotr Vechovensky. By inducing the young to follow Raskolnikov and throw aside all restraint in their personal behavior, the way is prepared for a corresponding lack of restraint in the exercise of power. "A generation or two of debauchery," Pyotr Vechovensky says, followed by "a little drop of nice fresh bloodletting just to accustom people," and "then the turmoil will begin." Today, a century later, it is well under way.

What Dostoevsky understood with such wonderful clarity is that the romantic notions of old Vechovensky are the inevitable prelude to the devilish ones of his son Pyotr, and that both derive from one of Geneva's favorite sons, Jean-Jacques Rousseau, who insisted that men

---

*In Constance Garnett's famous translation, the title is given as *The Possessed*, possibly an unconscious effort to tone down Dostoevsky's savagely satirical presentation of the rage and destructiveness innate in the liberal mind.

can only be free when they do what they like, and that
doing what they like is conducive to their individual and
collective happiness, peace and security. Exactly the opposite, Dostoevsky insists, is the case; when men are
dominated by their own desires, they fall into the most
terrible of all servitudes. Young Vechovensky is simply
old Vechovensky writ large. The old one is serious and
foolish, the young one is frivolous and merciless, and after them both comes inexorably the Gadarene rush over
the cliff.

Old Vechovensky is a marvelous piece of character-
ization, immensely funny, and in his own way, immensely
touching. How often such voices as his have been heard
in Geneva, calling for peace, for liberty, for democracy.
He is Eleanor Roosevelt, he is Bertrand Russell, he is every siren voice urging us to follow Pyotr Vechovensky,
whose purpose is to hand us over to the sloganeers, the
brainwashers, the dogmatists, from whom there can be
no escape. And have we not seen the fulfillment of their
plans in, for instance, Germany's Baader-Meinhof Gang,
with Sartre as spokesman for the intelligentsia, throwing
in his blessing?

With *The Devils* out of the way, Dostoevsky knew
that the book he projected next could be written only in
Russia, and it was with infinite relief and delight that he
and Anna made arrangements to return there after their

long and troubled exile. They arrived back in St. Petersburg in the summer of 1871, with ten years, the most fruitful and serene of his life, before them. Thanks to Anna's careful management, they were able to acquire a house in Staraya Russa, an ancient town in Novgorod Province, and in its tranquility he wrote *A Raw Youth*, worked on *The Brothers Karamazov* and prepared his Pushkin Memorial speech. There is a description of the town in *The Brothers Karamazov*, and he imagined that from his window he could see the old white monastery where Alyosha was a monk and Father Zossima died.

Before starting work seriously on *The Brothers Karamazov* in the spring of 1878, Dostoevsky paid a visit to Optina Pustin monastery in the neighborhood of Tula and the family estate where his father had been murdered by the serfs. He stayed there two days and had several conversations with the saintly Father Ambrosius, the original for Father Zossima in *The Brothers Karamazov*. Many years later Tolstoy visited Optina Pustin on his last tragic journey, which ended in the stationmaster's house at Astapova. Both Tolstoy and Dostoevsky, in their different ways, were fascinated by monasticism, which has now, in the old traditional sense, been ended in Russia, though many of the monasteries themselves – for instance, Novo-Devichy, on the outskirts of Moscow –

have been painstakingly preserved and restored as national monuments, to be stared at by tourists, and perhaps one day, as Christians may dream, to receive back their monks.

Dostoevsky was a God-possessed man if there ever was one, as is clear in everything he wrote and in every character he created. All his life he was questing for God, and found Him – if indeed he ever did other than fitfully – only at the end of his days, after passing through what he called "the hell-fire of doubt." Freedom to choose between Good and Evil he saw as the very essence of earthly existence; better even to choose Evil than to have no choice. The Devil, he insists, has a necessary role in our human drama, though without him there can be contentment and well-being of a kind, amounting to Tolstoy's dream of happiness in earthly, mortal terms, which was to Dostoevsky deeply abhorrent. This is the dream, too, of all authoritarians, temporal and ecclesiastical, especially the latter, as Dostoevsky explains in one of his most famous passages – Ivan Karamazov's account to his brother Alyosha of an imaginary encounter between the Grand Inquisitor and the returned Christ in sixteenth-century Seville.

Christ has reappeared among the people and been recognized; he has performed miracles as he did in Galilee...

In his infinite mercy he once more walked among men in the semblance of man. The people are drawn to him by an irresistible force, they surround him, they throng about him, they follow him. He walks among them in silence with a gentle smile of infinite compassion. The sun of love burns in his heart, rays of light, of enlightenment, and of power stream from his eyes, and, pouring over the people, stir their hearts with responsive love. He stretches forth his hands to them, blesses them, and a healing virtue comes from contact with him, even from his garments…

Then, in the Cathedral of Seville, he raises from the dead a small girl who has been brought in for burial. Just as she is sitting up in her coffin and looking around her with surprise in her smiling eyes – just at that moment…

…the Cardinal himself, the Grand Inquisitor, passes by the cathedral in the square. He is an old man of nearly ninety, tall and erect, with a shriveled face and sunken eyes from which, though, a light like a fiery spark still gleams…He stops in front of the crowd and watches from a distance. He sees everything…and his face darkens. He knits his gray beetling brows and his eyes flash with an ominous fire. He stretches forth his finger and commands the guard to seize *him*…The guards take the prisoner to the dark, narrow, vaulted prison in the old building of the Sacred Court and lock him in there. The day passes and night falls, the dark, hot and breathless Seville night. The air is heavy with the scent of laurel and lemons. Amid the profound darkness the iron door of the prison is suddenly opened and the old

Grand Inquisitor himself slowly enters the prison with a light in his hand. He is alone and the door at once closes behind him. He stops in the doorway and gazes for a long time, for more than a minute, into his face. At last he approaches him slowly, puts the lamp on the table and says to him: Is it you? *You?*

The terrible burden that Christ had laid on mankind, the Grand Inquisitor explains, was freedom. When in the wilderness the Devil offered deliverance from this burden, the offer was recklessly rejected. Thus, Christ refused to turn stones into bread, thereby abolishing hunger; refused also to jump from a high pinnacle in the Temple to create wonder and awe, thereby attracting people to him and his cause; and finally refused to take over the kingdoms of the earth, which would have put him in a position to create earthly paradises everywhere. He even, for the sake of freedom, insisted on dying himself. However, quite soon after his death his Church decided to close with the Devil's offer, and in place of freedom provided miracles, mystery and authority – in contemporary terms, affluence, the marvels of science and an all-powerful state – to the very great betterment of the human condition. If now Christ remained in the world, he would upset everything again with this terrible, devastating, sublime freedom of his. So again he must die.

All the time the Grand Inquisitor has been speaking, Christ has remained quite silent, as on a previous occasion before Caiaphas, saying not a word.

> The Grand Inquisitor saw that the Prisoner had been listening intently to him all the time, looking gently into his face and evidently not wishing to say anything in reply. The old man would have liked him to say something, however bitter and terrible. But he suddenly approached the old man and kissed him gently on his bloodless, aged lips. That was all his answer. The old man gave a start. There was an imperceptible movement at the corners of his mouth; he went to the door and opened it and said to him: "Go, and come no more – don't come at all – never, never!" And he let him out into the dark streets and lanes of the city.

The Prisoner went away, leaving the old man with that kiss glowing in his heart. And so it glows still.

The statue in Moscow of Russia's national poet, Pushkin, was unveiled in June 1880, providing Dostoevsky with the opportunity he had long sought to speak to his fellow countrymen – to exhort them like the prophets of old; to warn them of the dangers that lay ahead, and of the ruinous consequences that would surely ensue if they followed the Westernizers with their fraudulent promises of progress and freedom. Now, seemingly, everything that Dostoevsky most abhorred has come to pass in Russia. The institutions on which he pinned his hopes – the monarchy and the Church – have collapsed, the one abolished and the other a shadow of itself; the Revolution he so dreaded has happened, and the Westerners may be said to have triumphed in the sense that industrialization, science and agnosticism are now the order of the day.

Dostoevsky's great moment came on the third day of the Pushkin celebrations. He delivered his address in the Hall of Columns, which was largely used in those days by the nobility for social occasions and to receive the Imperial Family. Forty-four years later, its name changed to the House of Trade Unions; Lenin's body was to lie in state there. One may imagine the scene – Dostoevsky, a truly prophetic figure, bearded, wild-eyed, his brow furrowed, and speaking (though from a prepared text) with great force and eloquence, and leading up to his tremendous climax when he proclaimed the coming of a universal brotherhood brought about, not by socialism and revolution, but by the full and perfect realization of "this Christian enlightenment of ours."

In the serener circumstances of his last years, Dostoevsky's essential love of life and joy in all God's creation found a surer expression than ever before. "Beauty," he makes Dmitri Karamazov – perhaps his favorite of the three brothers – say, "is not only a terrible, it is also a mysterious thing. There God and the Devil strive for mastery, and the battleground is the heart of men."

Almost exactly half a century ago, I was passing through St. Petersburg – or Leningrad, as it was called then – and some impulse led me to seek out Dostoevsky's grave. I found it with some difficulty, and stood by it for a while, thinking of this great writer, and of the extraordinary range of his genius and depths of his insights, and how his works, far from seeming to belong to a vanished past, grow ever more relevant to the dilemmas and distractions that are part of the experience of living in this world at any time and in any circumstances.

I was much younger then, of course, in sight of the beginning of a life, as now of its ending; in the intervening years a great deal has happened to the world, to Dostoevsky's reputation, and, for that matter, to me. Yet I still find myself marveling, as I did on that occasion, at how one man's genius can, as it were, pick up all the strands of an age, revealing its pattern – all its absurdity, all its diabolism and all its splendor. All the world in a grain of sand, Blake said; yes, and all of life in a word.

On the first occasion that I visited Dostoevsky's grave, it had an air of neglect. Today this is far from being the case. His reputation in his native Russia, after some ups and downs, stands higher than ever. His books are published in editions, not of tens but of hundreds of thousands; every word he wrote is piously preserved, studied and commented upon – sometimes, I daresay, in ways that would surprise him. All this would be a source of great satisfaction to him. His love for his native Russia was one of the few wholly consistent themes of his life. Abroad, he was always homesick, and his faith that somehow Russia and the Russian people had some special role to fulfill in the working out of the world's destiny never wavered, and only burnt brighter as the years passed.

Standing beside Dostoevsky's grave, it is impossible for me not to think of another of which I also have very vivid memories. I mean, of course, Tolstoy's at Yasnaya Polyana, on a ridge overlooking the forest in which, he was told as a child, a green stick was buried inscribed with the secret of everlasting happiness. Tolstoy never did find that green stick, and Dostoevsky never even looked for it; yet somehow these two great Russian writers seem linked together. In life, as it happened, whether by accident or deliberation, they never actually met. But certainly they took great account of one another's works – Tolstoy aspiring so ardently after his kingdom of heaven on earth and arriving at Astapova; Dostoevsky plunging down so frenziedly into his kingdom of hell on earth and arriving at Golgotha – two parallel lines that Euclid told us never meet, but which, it has now been discovered, after all, do. It is where they meet that we mortals must live.

leo tolstoy

1828 — 1910

Contrary to the expectations of Marx, Engels and other pundits, the first rumblings of a new age of revolution were to be heard in distant, backward Russia. And it was the great Russian novelist Count Leo Tolstoy who, as it turned out, detected and responded to them most perceptively.

Like Augustine confronted with the fall of Rome, Tolstoy set himself to defend the Christian faith in order that it might survive the troubled years that lay ahead. Where Augustine shored up a Church, Tolstoy turned to the Gospels themselves, in his own words and stories beautifully expounding their message of the Kingdom of Heaven within us.

In Tolstoy's case, the miracle is clear for all to see. After more than half a century of authoritarian government bent on extirpating the Christian religion and all its work, Christ is alive in Russia as nowhere else. For this, the works of Tolstoy are in a large part responsible; Alexander Solzhenitsyn stands on his shoulders.

In November 1910, all eyes were fixed on the station-master's house in Astapova, a tiny place in eastern Russia, where Tolstoy lay dying. He was in his eighties and in flight from his home and his wife; concerned to start a new life in this world, just at the point of his departure from it. The whole Tolstoy clan had arrived by special train, including his abandoned wife, the Countess Sonya. Cameras – a relatively new feature of news-gathering – were out in strength, including one for movies.

In accordance with his wishes, Tolstoy was buried at Yasnaya Polyana, his family estate. The place he chose for his grave was on the edge of a ravine in the Zakaz forest; a ravine where, as his brother Nicholas used to say, a little green stick was hidden with the secret of universal love engraved on it.

There could have been no more suitable place. Tolstoy, it is true, never found the green stick, though he hunted assiduously for it. He did, however, find the secret of universal love – in the New Testament, especially in the Sermon on the Mount, whose sublime propositions he extolled and explained in his writings, and ardently tried to live by himself, insisting that they alone would

save men from the conflicts and upheavals which otherwise lay ahead.

It was this insistence that Christianity was not just a
religion but a way of life which made Tolstoy so revered
a figure throughout the world, while at the same time
making him seem – in the eyes of the civil authorities – a
dangerous revolutionary, and – in the eyes of the ecclesiastical authorities – a dangerous heretic. The sufferings of the poor, the afflicted and the oppressed; the
futility of trying to find fulfillment through the senses,
or celebrity, or any of the pursuits of the will or the ego;
the inadequacy of power as an instrument for instituting
justice and brotherliness – all this was made actual by
the light of his genius and the force of his sincerity.

I was seven years old when Tolstoy died in 1910. In
my home his name was honored, and as a child I stayed
for a while in a now defunct Tolstoyan colony in the
Cotswolds, near Stroud in Gloucestershire. His books
were all in my father's library, and I remember turning
over their pages even before I could properly read them.

I imagine Tolstoy looking across the ravine where the
little green stick is hidden, whose inscription must forever be sought and yet is forever known. What is it?
That we must love and not persecute or kill or wreak
vengeance upon one another. That, being part of one

Creation, with one Creator, we must seek our happiness in the good of others, thereby realizing our own good and living like brothers in one human family.

Tolstoy went on revealing the secret of universal love to his readers until the end of his life, even in the very last words that he wrote, but adding, most movingly: "That is what I wanted to say to you, my brothers, before I died." He is saying it still.

It was not, then, just because Tolstoy was a great writer that all eyes were fixed on the Astapova railway station when he lay dying there, nor was it just curiosity about the strange departure of a famous old man from his home and wife in order to become a solitary wanderer.

There was something else. The drama of his life was somehow that of the age, and as such it held everyone's attention. In this sense his own life was his greatest production – more so even than his supreme masterpiece *War and Peace*, or *Anna Karenina* and *Resurrection*. It began, as it ended, in Yasnaya Polyana.

Tolstoy has written, in glowing terms, his own, thinly disguised account of his childhood, boyhood, and youth. The only comparable descriptions of growing up that I can think of are Dickens's *David Copperfield* and Rousseau's *Confessions*, both books known to have impressed Tolstoy. The mood of each of them is nostalgic; a song of innocence written in the light of experience.

Even discounting all this, one can see that Yasnaya Polyana, as Tolstoy knew it, must have been the perfect place in which for him to grow up. It is true that his mother died before he could know her, and his father when he was only eight, but there were aunts and a grandmother to look after the children, a kindly, absurd German tutor to give them lessons, an array of servants to serve and scold them, and animals of all kinds to ride and take out for walks and keep as pets.

From a very early age Tolstoy seems to have been aware that he was an exceptional person. "Once and for all," he wrote in his diary, "I must become accustomed to the thought that I am an exception, and that either I am ahead of my age, or one of those incompatible, unadaptable natures that are never satisfied." In point of fact, though he did not realize it at the time, and perhaps never did, he was both ahead of his age and never satisfied.

In any case, his upbringing was calculated to foster all that was original and audacious and inspired in him: the very elements of his genius. His submission to the dreary treadmill of education – that conspiracy of dullness and futility, as he described it – was minimal. At Kazan University, which he and his brothers attended, his performance was scandalously desultory and he left without being graduated.

Later, when he decided to take his duties as a land-owner seriously, he turned his attention to educating the children of his serfs. With his usual ardor, he set up schools on the estate he had inherited, took on teaching duties, and carefully explored all the new educational theories and permissive practices, mostly derived from Germany, which have become all too lamentably familiar in our own time.

He was, it should be said, a marvelous teacher, and produced a number of highly effective textbooks. All his life he adored children, and was a master at devising and telling them stories. In the end, however, he came to see that education, like the Kingdom of Heaven, is within us, and cannot be imposed from without, however ingenious the theory or enlightened the teacher. When he talked with the old, uneducated *muzhiks* (peasants), he found that they were often wiser, and more in touch with the realities of our human existence than were their children who had passed through his schools.

It is often supposed that Tolstoy's distaste for worldly pursuits and ways only developed in middle age. This is not, in fact, so. From his earliest writings and journals it is clear that he alternated between an ardent delight in such things as social success and fame, and an equally passionate loathing of himself for so caring about them. This applied particularly to his love affairs and frequen-

tation of the gypsies; even more so to sordid episodes
like visits to brothels. He described one such visit and the
revulsion he experienced with great feeling.

By the time he was twenty-three, he had already tired
of social life in Moscow, and found an escape in going to
the Caucasus with his beloved brother, Nicholas, whose
battery was stationed there. He found the scenery marvelous, the Cossack women entrancing, and military life
very much to his taste.

In many ways the profession of arms appealed to
Tolstoy. The quality it most demanded, courage, was
one by which he himself set great store, and the alterna-
tions of danger and austerity with wild living suited his
temperament. As he demonstrated in *War and Peace*, he
had a masterly understanding of the conduct of battles
and campaigns. And even after he had become an out-
and-out pacifist, he would confide to his diary how
ashamed he was of the excitement and partisanship still
stirred up in him when Russia was at war.

Yet eventually this huntsman and soldier who gloried
in shedding blood became passionately convinced that
killing, either of men or of animals, could never be justified. Even when Tsar Alexander II was assassinated by
revolutionary terrorists in 1881, Tolstoy wrote to the new
tsar, Alexander III, pleading with him to spare the assas-
sins. Their ideas, Tolstoy contended, could be opposed

only by confronting them with forgiveness and love: "As wax before fire, every revolutionary struggle will melt away before the man-Tsar who fulfills the law of Christ."

Needless to say, the appeal went unheeded. As it turned out, the Tsar's policy could scarcely be said to have been particularly efficacious. Thirty-seven years later his dynasty was abolished, and the revolution Tolstoy had foreseen triumphed in Russia. Meanwhile, in far-off India, a barrister named Gandhi had noted Tolstoy's point, and acting on it, spearheaded a movement of nonviolent civil disobedience that ultimately succeeded in ending British rule in India.

It was while he was in the Caucasus that Tolstoy began to write in a serious way. His first published work, *Childhood*, was an instantaneous success. Yet neither then nor subsequently did his success as a writer bring him any lasting satisfaction. It might almost be said that for him writing was a sort of therapy. By recording, as he did with such incomparable brilliance, his impressions of life, he was able to escape temporarily from his everlasting preoccupation with its meaning. Or, put another way, he lived so intensely when he wrote that he could momentarily forget he must die.

Even in these early days Tolstoy found himself driven to the conclusion that the reality of life was essentially spiritual, and that it was best experienced not egotistically, but through a brotherly relationship with one's fellow men. Thus began his lifelong battle with his deeply sensual nature and with the habits and aptitudes of the class into which he had been born. He longed to escape from the urges of his flesh and from the privileges and tastes that his birth had conferred upon him. As a member of a tiny elite concerned with its own status, its own notions of art, and its own luxurious and self-indulgent way of life, he felt cut off from the great mass of mankind, symbolized for him by a decidedly idealized Russian *muzhik*.

To Tolstoy's considerable chagrin, the family regularly went in convoy from Yasnaya Polyana to Moscow, for the children to go to school there, and for Sonya to taste the pleasures of social life and musical occasions. It was the sort of thing that produced a frenzy of irritation in Tolstoy, but Sonya was in her element. Relations between them were often strained. The sort of people who came to Sonya's receptions were, for the most part, unsympathetic to Tolstoy, who longed for his rides and walks and meditations in the woods at Yasnaya Polyana. The Moscow house itself was an old, wood one which had escaped the great fire so vividly described in *War and Peace*. In his time, for a town residence, it was relatively isolated, which pleased Tolstoy.

In dwelling on the darker side of the Tolstoys' marriage, it is often forgotten how idyllically happy it was in its first years. Despite the strife and misunderstandings and bitterness, the bond between them survived to the end, and beyond. Sonya lived on to witness the October Revolution. When in 1919, her daughter Tanya asked her if she often thought of Tolstoy, she answered that she never thought about anything else. "I have never stopped living by his side," she said, "and I torment myself because I was not good. However, I was always faithful to him, body and soul."

Sonya was only eighteen when she married Tolstoy in 1862; he was thirty-four. The wedding took place in the Church of the Nativity in the Kremlin, where Sonya's father was resident doctor to the administrative staff. For Tolstoy, it was the end of the womanizing which had hitherto played so large and troubling a part in his life. Though sorely tempted at times, he remained true to his marriage vows.

Characteristically, he felt bound to show Sonya his private diary, which recorded his various love affairs, including one homosexual experience. On a young and innocent girl this was bound to have a devastating effect, which Tolstoy should have foreseen. Or was there perhaps some unconscious perversity in thus exposing himself? In any case, diaries of one sort or another were to haunt their lives.

It was during their first happy years together, when their children were being born and growing up, that Tolstoy's powers as a novelist were at their height. Sonya participated in his work, not just copying and recopying his numerous drafts, but making useful suggestions and corrections on her own. She rejoiced in his growing fame and success, and, humanly, in the greater affluence it provided for the family.

Serious troubles between them only began after Tolstoy's spiritual crisis. His Franciscan passion to live like the very poor and abstain from "all fleshly indulgence" went ill with the upper-class style of living Sonya had come to expect as her due; as it did with normal marital relations. An occasional reluctant surrender, followed by anguished remorse, was unlikely to appeal to any wife, least of all one as demanding and full of self-esteem as Sonya.

Things were made worse by some of the disciples and acolytes who flocked to Tolstoy in his new role as moralist and evangelist. Notably, Vladimir Chertkov, who achieved an ascendancy over Tolstoy and took over the publication of his works – a domain which Sonya considered peculiarly her own.

Chertkov seems to have been a pedantic, tiresome, boring sort of person, and Sonya hated him. Harking back to that first fatal showing of her husband's diary before their marriage, she even accused Tolstoy of having abnormal relations with Chertkov. The fact that she could make so preposterous a suggestion indicates the mixture of envy and jealousy which was to poison the rest of their life together.

Tolstoy, it must be admitted, never succeeded in wholly clarifying, to himself or to others, where he stood in this matter of sexual indulgence, and it is very easy to pull to pieces the various, extreme positions he took – as that the ideal that everyone should pursue is total abstinence, or that any indulgence other than for procreative purposes amounts to whoring. Yet we who are witnessing the appalling consequences of accepting promiscuity as normal human behavior may well pause before dismissing Tolstoy as a soured idealist and a crank. What he had to say on the subject, especially in a masterpiece like *Resurrection*, I confidently predict, will be respectfully regarded long after *Lady Chatterley's Lover* has been dismissed for its fathomless imbecility.

In his great novels *War and Peace* and *Anna Karenina*, Tolstoy always drew from life, and thus it is possible to identify the characters, as well as the buildings and places, where a scene is set. For instance, the building which now houses the headquarters of the Soviet Writers Union (a stronghold of literary orthodoxy), was the model for the Rostovs' Moscow house in *War and Peace*, just as Ilya Andreyevich Rostov himself was based on Tolstoy's paternal grandfather, Ilya Andreyevich Tolstoy.

Tolstoy did not believe in invention in art. The author, he considered, should not egotistically impose himself on his material. Likewise, in his use of history, he discounts the Nietzschean notion of great men dominating and shaping events. History, as he sees it, is a kind of cosmic soap-opera, an emanation of the collective consciousness which is played back to edify, instruct and entertain.

In *War and Peace*, it is the Russian general Kutusov who, as Tolstoy portrays him, allows himself to be the instrument, rather than the shaper, of historical forces, whereas his opponent, Napoleon, exemplifies the ego striving (vainly, as it turns out) to assert itself in domination over men and events. In such a conflict, Tolstoy indicates, Kutusov was bound to win – life being stronger than any ego, however puffed up.

In other words, even before his spiritual crisis, Tolstoy in his writings was pursuing an essentially moral purpose. Later, in his book *What is Art?*, he worked out in his own wayward, inimitable way, the theory of what was already his practice – that art should be a parable expounding life's goodness and truth and beauty in

terms comprehensible to everyone, not just to a special-
ized elite. After his spiritual crisis, his parables became
explicit (as in beautiful short stories like *Master and Man*
and *What Men Live By*, and in his play, *The Power of
Darkness*) whereas before they had been implicit.

Thus in *War and Peace* he explored power, the appetite
of the will, and in *Anna Karenina* carnality, the appetite
of the flesh; two passions whose destructive consequences he had experienced himself, especially the latter.
As *Anna Karenina* and *War and Peace* conveyed his own
involvement in these passions, he was not being hypo-
critical when he insisted that he looked back on the books
with distaste, and even wished he had not written them.
At the same time, he was perfectly well aware that
merely to have contented himself with writing a moral
treatise on the devastations of power on the collectivity,
and of carnality on the individual, would not have served
his purpose.

If, he once remarked in a letter to a friend, he were to be
told he could write a novel in which all his views on what
is socially right and just were to be irrefutably upheld, he
would not feel inclined to dedicate two hours to the task.
If, on the other hand, he were told that what he wrote
would be read twenty years later by those who were now
children, and that they would weep and laugh over it,

and fall in love with the life in it, then he would dedicate all his existence and powers to producing such a work.

He need not have worried. The twenty years have long since passed, and still we weep and laugh over his writings, and are entranced by the life in them that shines and dances like sunlight. So, we may be sure, it will continue.

In middle age Tolstoy experienced a spiritual crisis which was far and away the most important thing that ever happened to him, and which altered fundamentally the course of his life during his remaining thirty-odd years. As a writer he had achieved a position of eminence which would have enabled him, had he cared to, to turn into one of those men of letters who become public figures, appearing covered with decorations at banquets to deliver respectfully applauded, pontifical addresses.

Instead he found himself desperately trying to discover what, if anything, his life was about. In the writings of philosophers and moralists he could find no satisfaction. Egotistic and sensual pleasures merely repelled him. The two solaces he had looked to, a happy family life and artistic creation, no longer sufficed. As for the progress of mankind and his achieving fulfillment through promoting it – the very notion struck him as derisory. The only thing he knew for certain was that he must soon die. Why, then, wait?

In his *Confession* — a book that may be put beside Saint Augustine's — he described his predicament thus:

> I was happy, yet I hid away a cord to avoid being tempted to hang myself by it to one of the pegs between the cupboards of my study where I undressed alone every evening, and ceased carrying a gun because it offered too easy a way of getting rid of life. I knew not what I wanted, I was afraid of life; I shrank from it, and yet there was something I hoped for from it.

In this predicament, Tolstoy observed that only in his own tiny circle of the educated, rich and mostly idle, did people take so despairing a view of life. The others, the *muzhiks,* went about their work, got up in the morning and lay down at night with a sense that life was essentially good, however arduous and full of hardships it might be for them. Likewise, when the time came for them to die, they were ready to close their eyes and depart without fear or recrimination. They, who had so little and knew so little, were at peace with themselves and with the world; it was the others, who had so much and thought they knew so much, who despaired.

Wherein, then, he asked himself, did the difference lie? Clearly, in that the *muzhiks* had faith, which was something quite different from metaphysical conclusions, ethical propositions or epicurean pursuits. So Tolstoy sought to have faith himself. The rest of his life was dedicated to a quest for it, which meant, as he discovered, a quest for God. Every time he came within sight of God, he wrote, "again life flashed through my veins. All about me seemed to revive, to have a new meaning." When, for one reason or another, he found himself separated from God, all seemed to die around him and within him and again he wished to kill himself.

In his quest for faith, Tolstoy resumed the practice of the Russian Orthodox Church, in which he had been brought up; he attended services in the church where the people from Yasnaya Polyana came to worship and where numerous members of his family are buried. Observing fasts and other disciplines, making confessions to and receiving the ministrations of a simple priest, he was overjoyed to feel himself at one with the worshipers, whoever and whatever they might be.

Then doubts began to assail him. The attitudes of the Church, particularly towards war, its sycophantic relations with the government and acquiescence in all of the Tsar's policies, seemed to him in direct conflict with Christ's teaching. In consequence, its prayers, its ceremonies, the myths and superstitions it fostered, came to seem increasingly hollow and unconvincing. In voicing his doubts he came into conflict with the ecclesiastical authorities, and in the end an edict of the Holy Synod excommunicated him. The break was final.

Thenceforth, Tolstoy's quest for God was a lonely and solitary one, and, in the sense of providing him with a sure faith, unrealized. He struggled on doggedly and bravely, but he never found the enduring serenity and harmonious relationship with his family he so longed for. Cobbling shoes and dressing like a peasant did not make him one, no more than transferring his property to his children made him a pauper, or than the ardent practice of asceticism quenched his inexhaustible vitality and zest for living.

Yet his sense of the false direction the world was taking, and the false gods it was enthroning, has been amply justified by events. He saw with inspired clarity that without a sense of moral order there could be no order of any kind, and performed the inestimable service of warning future generations against involvement in the corruption of power and the smoke clouds of obscurantism, thereby enabling Christian faith to survive when those particular organs of power had been overthrown and those particular clouds dispersed.

The great Russian writer Maxim Gorky once said that Tolstoy was "like a great steeple whose bell is heard throughout the world." Many of those who responded to the bell, as Gorky went on to point out, were rather deplorable figures – scroungers, crackpots and eccentrics of all sorts and descriptions known in Yasnaya Polyana as the Dark Ones. Even Tolstoy was heard to speak disparagingly of the Tolstoyans. Yet he received them, one and all, believing that as they were his followers, he owed them a duty, and always hoping that underneath the strange behavior and outlandish clothing of one of them he would find a John the Baptist or Francis of Assisi.

His mail likewise came from all over the world. Letters asking for advice, arguing, advertising their writer, scolding Tolstoy or pleading with him to support this or that project. These, too, were all punctiliously dealt with. Then there were visiting celebrities, some of them American, who may well at the end of the day have proved more tedious and demanding than even the Dark Ones.

It was an endless procession, all equally bent on satisfying their curiosity and paying homage to this extraordinary man – this aristocrat who dressed like a *muzhik;* this famous writer who cobbled shoes; this ardent huntsman who could not endure the thought of shedding blood; this scholar who despised learning, envying peasants their simple faith, and calling upon a world rushing headlong in the direction of technology, affluence and the egotistical pursuit of happiness, to return to Christ's gospel of love, recognizing that "only the spirit gives life to man…Evil does not exist for the spirit, for it is but a counterfeit of life…He who possesses the life of the spirit has eternal life."

There were few who heeded his words, but everyone listened, because they knew in their hearts that what he said was true. He was, in the old Russian sense, a *Starets*, a Holy Man, having some special relationship with life – the trees, the wind, the toil and passions of men – whereby he understood its true nature.

Since family life at Yasnaya Polyana should have been, in accordance with Tolstoy's ideas, harmonious and happy, it was a source of grief to him that in practice it was often full of strife and misery. In his later years there was a running quarrel between him and his wife, sometimes flaring up into theatrical scenes and rows, sometimes just smoldering, but only rarely quiescent.

The whole Tolstoy family – father, mother, children, aunts, uncles – were inveterate keepers of diaries. Even visitors were infected with the habit. One has the sense that, after lights-out at Yasnaya Polyana, everyone scampered off to write in their diaries, or to take a surreptitious look at someone else's. Tolstoy himself, besides his own private journal to which his wife had access – indeed, he sometimes used it to convey messages to her – kept another, most-secret one, which itself became a source of more quarrels. This was surely the best documented domestic scene in all history!

Tolstoy's scathing attacks on the institution of property made it humiliating for him to be a landowner, and his constant exhortations in favor of sexual abstinence embarrassed his wife, especially when she found herself pregnant for the thirteenth time.

In neither case was there any element of hypocrisy on Tolstoy's part. He genuinely longed to get rid of his property, as he did to be delivered from his sexual appetites, but in the one instance his family responsibilities stood in the way; and in the other stood his sensuality, which continued to assail him even as an old man. Like King Lear he did in fact divide up his property among his children (which, incidentally, may explain why he so inordinately disliked Shakespeare's play, seeing himself, perhaps, in the distracted old king), but this still left the vexing question of his immensely profitable writings. In the end, a compromise of sorts was worked out, whereby his wife had the copyright of his early works, and his later religious writings were available to anyone who cared to publish them. The royalties of *Resurrection*, which had an enormous sale all over the world, he turned over to a religious sect, the Dukhobors, to help them settle in Canada in order to avoid military conscription, which they considered sinful.

Tolstoy's anguish over these unhappy circumstances did not lead him for a single moment to doubt the conclusions he had reached about the validity of Christ's teaching. He knew quite well, and never tired of saying (notably, in his book *The Kingdom of God Is within You*) that the perfection envisaged in the Gospels is unattainable in earthly terms, whether through good works or revolutionary changes. It is in aspiring after this perfection, as individual pilgrims passing through the world, that our intrinsically imperfect natures can be redeemed, he insisted, and the world be made a happier, more just and more brotherly place to live.

Tolstoy was such a pilgrim, one of the greatest, and like Bunyan's Pilgrim found himself distressed and fearful right at the end of his journey.

The incompatibility between himself and his wife, the rows they had about money, the publication of his books, and how they should live, made him feel more than ever that their life together had become impossible. For him the only necessities were simple clothes, a bare bedroom, and frugal food, while she pined for a social life. So, at the age of eighty-two, on October 28, 1910, he decided that his long struggle to reconcile their life together with how he thought they should live could no longer be continued at Yasnaya Polyana. In a farewell note to his wife he wrote: "I am doing what people of my age often do — giving up the world in order to spend my last days alone and in silence."

Then he made off, accompanied only by his Yugoslav friend and doctor, Makovitsky – not, as he had hoped, to silence and solitude, but to a glare of publicity. Their strange, nightmarish journey ended at Astapova, where they got off the train because of Tolstoy's high temperature and generally sick condition. Previously, they had visited Tolstoy's sister Maria, a nun, at her convent, and Tolstoy had even considered staying at a nearby monastery on the characteristic condition that he should not be required to attend any religious services. At Astapova he was put to bed in the stationmaster's house, thus achieving at last his dream of living like a poor man – though even then the stationmaster insisted that Tolstoy have the best room.

As the news of Tolstoy's whereabouts became known, Astapova was, for a minute, the focus of the world's curiosity. Journalists arrived in hordes. The telephone in the stationmaster's office never stopped ringing. A special contingent of police were drafted on. Photographers clicked their cameras incessantly. Chertkov arrived, and a special train brought a large party of Tolstoyans, led by the Countess. As they all milled around, peering everywhere, questioning everyone, the trains came and went.

Only the center of all the interest, the shrunken old man lying in the stationmaster's house, seemed indifferent to it all. For him, at last, escape from the perplexities of life was near. He was dying, and imagined himself back in the little vaulted room at Yasnaya Polyana. Only this time, no rustling figure came peering in. His wife was kept away from him until the very last moment. The last clear words he was heard to utter were: "To seek, always to seek." One thinks again of King Lear:

> Vex not his ghost, O let him pass
> He hates him who would upon the rack
> Of this tough world
> Stretch him out longer.

The best description of Tolstoy that I ever read was by Maxim Gorky:

> I once saw him as, perhaps, no one has ever seen him. I was walking over to him at Gaspra along the coast, and behind Yessupov's estate, on the shore among the stones, I saw his smallish angular figure in a gray, crumpled, ragged suit and crumpled hat. He was sitting with his head on his hands, the wind blowing the silvery hairs of his beard through his fingers; he was looking into the distance out to sea, and the little greenish waves rolled up obediently to his feet and fondled them as though they were telling something about themselves to the old magician. It was a day of sun and cloud, and the shadows of the clouds glided over the stones, and with the stones the old man grew now bright and now dark. The boulders were large, riven by cracks, and covered with smelly seaweed; there had been a high

tide. He, too, seemed to me like an old stone come to life, who knows all the beginnings and the ends of things, who considers when and what will be the end of the stones, of the grasses of the earth, of the waters of the sea, and of the whole universe from the pebbles to the sun. And the sea is part of his soul, and everything around him comes from him, out of him. In the musing motionlessness of the old man I felt something fateful, magical, something which went down into the darkness beneath him and stretched up like a search-light, into the blue emptiness above the earth…In my soul there was joy and fear, and then everything blended in one happy thought: "I am not an orphan on the earth as long as this man lives on it."

Tolstoy's supreme genius has produced a surprising consequence more than half a century after his death, symbolized by bridal couples who come continuously from the nearby city of Tula to lay flowers on his grave at Yasnaya Polyana as part of their marriage ceremony, thereby setting a spiritual seal on a legal compact.

Throughout its existence the Soviet state has sought to abolish the Christian religion, using for the purpose its total control of whatever influences the minds and lives of its citizens. Yet as it turns out, all its efforts have been frustrated by the irresistible presentation of Christ and his teachings in Tolstoy's writings, which continue to be avidly read by his countrymen.

Tolstoy's parables are, to me, the most artistically beautiful and powerful in their impact since the original ones in the New Testament. So, by some great miracle, the promise in the first chapter of the fourth Gospel remains valid, even in the modern world's first overtly atheistic state. Thanks to Tolstoy, the Word goes on becoming flesh even there, full of grace and truth.

dietrich bonhoeffer

1906 — 1945

Our book ends where it began, with an earthly city in flames and a social order collapsing.

Instead of Rome, Berlin; instead of the Roman Empire, Hitler's Third Reich; instead of a professor of rhetoric who became a bishop, we have a Lutheran pastor imprisoned on charges of helping to plot a murder; a bourgeois German who found fulfillment among the lowest of the low; an erudite theologian who experienced the stupendous simplification of dying on a scaffold like his Master.

The formalities of admission were correctly completed. For the first night I was locked up in a holding cell. The blankets on the camp bed had such a foul smell that in spite of the cold it was impossible to use them. Next morning a piece of bread was thrown into my cell; I had to pick it up from the floor. The sound of the prison staff's vile abuse of the men who were held for investigation penetrated into my cell for the first time; since then, I have heard it every day from morning to night.

The first night I could sleep very little because a prisoner in the next cell wept loudly for several hours. Nobody took any notice.

In those first days of complete isolation I did not see anything of the actual life of the prison; I only formed a picture of what was going on from the almost uninterrupted shouting of the warders.

After twelve days the authorities got to know of my family connections. While this was, of course, a great relief for me personally, from an objective point of view it was most embarrassing to see how everything changed from that moment. I was put into a more spacious cell which was cleaned for me daily by one of the men. When the food came round I was offered larger rations. I always refused, since they would have been at the expense of other prisoners.

Thus Dietrich Bonhoeffer described his arrival in Tegel Prison, in Berlin, where he was to spend the months from April 5, 1943, to October 8, 1944. It was during this period that he wrote the *Letters and Papers from Prison*, which I, in common with many others, have found so helpful in confronting the spiritual dilemmas of our time. Bonhoeffer had been arrested and imprisoned for his participation in a plot to assassinate Adolf Hitler — an involvement deliberately chosen, and arguably misguided.

In prison, in the course of his voluminous correspondence, he sorted out his theological views, views which his closest associates consider to have been subsequently misinterpreted.

However, it was neither as a conspirator nor as a theologian that his memory was honored on July 27, 1945 by a congregation gathered in Holy Trinity Church, in war-scarred London, but rather as a Christian martyr whose steadfast faith was a bright light in a dark time.

"Let us pray. We are gathered here in the presence of God, to make thankful remembrance of the life and work of his servant Dietrich Bonhoeffer…"

It was these words, broadcast by the BBC in a memorial service for Bonhoeffer, that brought to his family in Berlin the first news of his death at the hands of the Nazis. Among the congregation at the memorial service were members of the Lutheran church in Sydenham, London, where for a time Bonhoeffer had served as pastor.

Bonhoeffer's pastorate in London enabled him to make personal contacts which served him well in his work for the resistance movement in Germany. When he was recruited into the *Abwehr*, or German intelligence service, he had occasion to travel to Switzerland and Stockholm, and to meet Christian leaders from enemy countries. Among them was Bishop Bell of Chichester, who delivered the address at Bonhoeffer's memorial service:

In this church, hallowed by many memories of Christian fellowship in wartime, we gather now in memory of Dietrich Bonhoeffer, our most dear brother and martyr of the Church.

He was born in Breslau on February 4, 1906, the son of a famous physician, and belonged to a family which claimed not a few eminent divines, judges, and artists in its ranks in previous generations.

Bonhoeffer's ancestors came from Schwäbisch-Hall, once a free city of Charlemagne's Holy Roman Empire, in the State of Wurtemberg. In the middle of the town there is a church full of memorials to the Bonhoeffer family, which for three centuries was prominent in its affairs. Free cities such as this one were doggedly tenacious of their independence, and it would not be fanciful to suggest that Dietrich Bonhoeffer's instinctive resistance to Nazi totalitarianism derived partly from his ancestry.

Bonhoeffer grew up in a comfortable middle-class family and moved in what now seems a protected, privileged environment, with all the qualities, prejudices and values such an upbringing bestows.

When Hitler became chancellor in 1933, Bonhoeffer understood at once the threat this posed to all the decencies of life. He saw that the intensifying persecution of the Jews under the Nazi regime was not just abhorrent in human terms, but a deliberate attack on Christ Himself.

In 1933 Bonhoeffer visited Bethel, a famous settlement for the afflicted, near the Westphalian town of Bielefeld. His mind was greatly troubled by what he considered to be the indecision and confused thinking of many of his fellow pastors about the Nazi regime. Indeed, he had come to Bethel with a view to preparing a definitive confession of faith, which was in due course drafted, though not to his satisfaction. Friedrich von Bodelschwingh, the youngest son of Bethel's founder, was in charge and showed Bonhoeffer around. Von Bodelschwingh was himself closely associated with the Confessional Church – the breakaway Lutherans who refused to fall in with the requirements of the Nazi regime.

The experience comforted and reassured Bonhoeffer. It brought him into first-hand contact with the central fact of suffering in the world, and the question of how a Christian should respond to it – something of more fundamental importance to his life even than the abominations of National Socialism, or the equivocations and timidities of the Lutheran Church in the face of them.

Here were these broken, stumbling bodies, these wandering, vacant minds. Yet under loving care and guidance, they were capable of making a life together and worshiping together, perhaps with an enhanced sense of God's loving kindness, and of the joy of participating in His Creation. Bonhoeffer recalled that the Buddha is said to have been converted by contact with a sick person. Maybe in their total defenselessness, the afflicted of Bethel had a clearer sense of the essential defenselessness of our human condition than many who were whole and healthy – just as those who looked after them were brought nearer to God through the experience.

While he was in Bethel, Bonhoeffer's mind naturally turned towards the infamous Nazi euthanasia laws, which legalized the elimination of what were considered to be useless lives. After all, the projected victims were all around him; he could watch them at work, and hear their songs. It was quite clear to him that a mindset whereby the sick and infirm could be disposed of was far more barbarous a sickness than any they had to deal with at Bethel.

As it happened, Hitler's euthanasia laws never were applied at Bethel – the single exception in the whole Reich. Von Bodelschwingh resolutely refused to provide the requisite information, and, when challenged, demonstrated conclusively that at Bethel there were no useless lives. The most stricken inmates could still communicate, if not in words, then in God's language of love. The body and the mind might be maimed, but the soul remained intact. Bonhoeffer was able to invoke the help of his father, who as an eminent neurologist, provided expert support for von Bodelschwingh's contention.

How ironic that now, after defeating the Nazis at so heavy a cost, similar euthanasia laws are being ardently recommended in the victor nations — on "humanitarian" grounds. If this should truly come to pass, then the darkness will indeed have fallen on Christendom's two thousand years.

The Nuremberg stadium, now derelict and deserted, remaining full of sinister memories for people of my generation, was Hitler's favorite set for mounting celebrations of Nazi power. As his position grew stronger the rallies developed into mere assertions of a collective will, with no other justification, no other coherent purpose, than its own glorification. It was a sort of crazy revivalist meeting, with all the familiar accompaniments of mass hysteria and shouting in unison — not to the glory of God, but of the Prince of Darkness.

This was what Bonhoeffer had to face. And as he said, it was not a case just of a deluded, vainglorious Germany. A sick man was in charge of a sick nation in a sick world.

From the beginning it was perfectly clear to Bonhoeffer that the Lutheran Church, as such, could have no lot or part in rendering what was claimed to be due to such a Caesar as this. Never for one moment did he, as a Lutheran pastor, countenance the notion of coming to terms with Nazi power.

His own position was the classic pacifist one. As late as 1934, at the Fanö ecumenical conference, he delivered a powerful address in the course of which he said, "Which of us can say he knows what it might mean to the world if one nation should meet the aggressor not with weapons in hand, but defenseless, praying, and for that very reason protected by a 'bulwark never failing'?"

Now he had to ask himself whether this Gandhi-like position could be seriously and honorably maintained, not just against an already crumbling British raj, but against the Great Beast which is unleashed when men turn inexorably away from God and surrender themselves to the darkest impulses of their human wills.

It always seems to me that it falls to some men to act out inside themselves the drama of the collectivity. They are not necessarily the most subtle or perceptive, or intelligent, but they have this special destiny. Bonhoeffer, with his somewhat ponderous, theologically oriented mind, with his full equipment of the inborn values and loyalties of his class and upbringing, was being edged, inch by inch, into such a position: into becoming an authentic hero of his time.

In Bethel the doctors and nurses and the Christian helpers would go on tending the epileptics and the sick. For Bonhoeffer now this was not enough.

Before the mounting hysterical ferocity of that terrible voice, and of the even more terrible regimented roar which answered, sounding out from the Nuremburg stadium through Germany and through the world, he felt it was not enough just to pray, just to fulfill his Christian duty to care for the afflicted. With increasing insistence, it was being pressed upon him that he would have to act.

Naturally, his chief concern was for his church, whose clergy were dangerously split between those who were prepared to make their terms with the Nazi regime, and the others, like Bonhoeffer, who refused to accept any doctrinal or other concessions to Hitler's Nietzschean ideology. For that reason, Bonhoeffer instituted clandestine seminaries at Zingst and Finkenwalde, where pastors could be trained capable of preaching and upholding the true gospel of Christ without reference to the moral and spiritual degradation which had befallen their country. It was the first step in his involvement in active opposition to Hitler, an involvement which was to make of him first a conspirator and then a martyr.

At this time Bonhoeffer became friendly with Eberhard Bethge, one of his seminarians, who was later to marry his niece Renate Schleicher and become his most intimate associate, confidante, and his definitive biographer. Without Bethge we would be without much essential information about Bonhoeffer, as well as the bulk of the *Letters from Prison*, which were addressed to Bethge.

Despite Bonhoeffer's work with his seminarians, family ties remained strong. Next door to the Bonhoeffers' house in Berlin lived Renate's parents, and whenever an opportunity offered they all met as of old. Another link was soon to manifest itself – their joint participation in a growing resistance movement against the Nazi regime. Here the leading figures were Bonhoeffer's brother-in-law Rüdiger Schleicher, his brother Klaus, and another brother-in-law, Hans von Dohnanyi. Like Bonhoeffer, all would be executed by the Nazis.

In 1939, just before the outbreak of war, Bonhoeffer spent time in New York City. He was strongly pressed to stay there, but all his own inclinations were the other way. "I must live through this difficult period of our national history with the Christian people of Germany," he wrote. "I shall have no right to participate in the reconstruction of Christian life in Germany after the war if I do not share the trials of this time with my people." So he returned. Had he stayed, America might have gained a theologian, but the world would have lost a martyr.

In conversations with me, Eberhard Bethge pointed out that there were three times in Bonhoeffer's life when he wanted to extricate himself from a particular situation, only to discover that thereby he would have lost, not gained, his freedom, and that the only way to keep his freedom was to stifle the impulse to make off. The first occasion was in 1933, when he went to a parish in London, but decided that his presence was needed with his theological students in Germany; the second was in 1939, when he made the dramatic decision to return from America to be with his own people in the tragic times he saw ahead. The last was when he could have escaped from prison with the connivance of the guards, but refrained because it would have endangered his brother and uncle, who were also in prison. In short, he was a man with a strong desire to escape, but in order to keep his freedom, he deliberately chose to stay put.

We went on to discuss the question of Bethge's and Bonhoeffer's participation in the plot to assassinate Hitler. This must have been a difficult decision for them both to make, I said. Bethge replied that curiously enough it wasn't. They didn't even discuss the matter, but just assumed as a matter of course that as followers of Christ, they could not possibly allow themselves to become accomplices in the slaughter of Jews and all the other horrible things that were going on in Germany. As Bethge put it, they had to make a stand, and they could not say, "You, Hans Dohnanyi, and you, Oster, you generals…do the really dirty work, and [we, as Christians], will do something just a little bit dirty." No, there had to be total commitment, total solidarity and true loyalty to their comrades who were not in a position to plead that, being ministers, they really did not engage in such practices. Thus, even in prison, Bonhoeffer had to continue with the double life which had begun while he was ostensibly working for the *Abwehr* and actually furthering the conspiracy. In order to safeguard friends outside prison who were keeping the conspiracy going, Bonhoeffer had to purport to be a good Nazi and true patriot, though it meant betraying his own earlier sayings to the contrary.

Bonhoeffer's involvement in the assassination plot against Hitler developed while he was staying at a Benedictine monastery at Ettal, whose monks and way of life were very dear to him. The next step was for him to be taken into the *Abwehr*, ostensibly to be a courier whose job would be to find out about the ecumenical movement. This enabled him to meet Bishop Bell who, in his memorial service described what happened when he and Bonhoeffer met in Stockholm:

> It was in May 1942 that I had my last sight of him in Stockholm, when, altogether unexpectedly, he came from Berlin at the risk of his life to give me much information of the utmost importance about the movement of the opposition in Germany to eliminate Hitler and all his chief colleagues, and to set up a new government which should repeal the Nuremberg Laws, undo Hitler's deeds so far as

they could be undone, and seek peace with the Allies. Of those solemn last talks I had with Dietrich I will say nothing further but this: deeply committed as he was to the plan for elimination, he was not altogether at ease as a Christian about such a solution. "There must be punishment by God," he said. "We do not want to escape repentance. The elimination itself," he urged, "must be understood as an act of repentance. Oh, we have to be punished, Christians do not wish to escape repentance or chaos, if God wills to bring it on us. We must endure this judgement as Christians." Very moving was our talk; very moving our farewell. And the last letter I had from him, just before he returned to Berlin, knowing what might well await him there, I shall treasure for the whole of my life.

Not many months after his return he was arrested.

It is an awesome thought that the eighteen months or so that Bonhoeffer spent as a prisoner in Tegel Prison was spiritually the richest, and intellectually and artistically the most fertile, period of his life. All his circumstances prior to his imprisonment were conducive to him becoming a useful and enlightened citizen. Indeed, he had already become a pillar of the Confessional Church – a teacher, preacher and scholar of growing renown, inside Germany and abroad. All this (and I do not mean it disparagingly at all) was to be expected from so honorable and honest a product of a God-fearing, cultivated, upper-middle-class home.

In his cell, however, the theologian became a mystic, the pastor became a martyr, and the teacher produced, in his *Letters and Papers from Prison,* one of the great contemporary classics of Christian literature. It is very difficult indeed for a twentieth-century mind to accept, or even grasp, the notion of the blessedness of affliction. Bonhoeffer provides us with a perfect object lesson. His greatness grew directly out of his affliction, and through the very hopelessness of his earthly state, he was able to generate hope at a dark moment in history, when it was most sorely needed, comforting and heartening many.

When Bonhoeffer heard in prison that the plot of July 1944 had failed, he realized that Hitler, having miraculously survived the assassination attempt, would be merciless in liquidating the conspirators. Now he knew that, in human terms, their cause was lost. God had overruled their earthly purpose, and nothing remained for him but to come to terms, once and for all, with the Cross. In the plot's failure lay his triumph, as in losing his life he would gain it. This is beautifully conveyed in his last writings in prison.

I have never regretted my decision in the summer of 1939 to return to Germany, for I'm firmly convinced – however strange it may seem – that my life has followed a straight and unbroken course, at any rate in its outward conduct. It has been an uninterrupted enrichment of experience, for which I can only be thankful. If I were to end my life here in these conditions, that would have a meaning that I think I could understand.

Another thought he wrote down when he was in prison, one that I like very much, is this: "Death is the supreme festival on the road to freedom."

Despite the many things he says about himself in his *Letters*, Bonhoeffer was an extremely reticent person and rarely disclosed his profoundest feelings. But in this letter of August 1944, the last one he wrote to Bethge, he said:

> Please don't ever get anxious or worried about me, but don't forget to pray for me – I'm sure you don't. I am so sure of God's guiding hand that I hope I shall always be kept in that certainty. You must never doubt that I'm travelling with gratitude and cheerfulness along the road where I'm being led. My past life is brim-full of God's goodness, and my sins are covered by the forgiving love of Christ crucified. Forgive my writing this. Don't let it grieve or upset you for a moment, but let it make you happy. But I did want to say it for once, and I could not think of anyone else who I could be sure would take it aright.

Later in the same letter he goes on to refer to his young and very beautiful fiancée, Maria von Wedemeyer.

"Maria," he wrote, "was here today, so fresh and at the same time steadfast and tranquil in a way I've rarely seen."

In October, 1944, when further details of Bonhoeffer's conspiratorial activities were discovered, he was moved from Tegel to the Gestapo prison in Prinz-Albrecht-Strasse. The following February he was transferred to Buchenwald. Maria was somehow guided by instinct to follow him there, and then on to Flossenbürg. The last letter she got from him was for Christmas, 1944.

> These will be quiet days in our homes, but I have had the experience over and over again that the quieter it is around me, the clearer do I feel the connection to you. It is as though in solitude the soul develops senses which we hardly know in everyday life. Therefore I have not felt lonely or abandoned for one moment. You must not think that I am unhappy. What is happiness and unhappiness? It depends so little on the circumstances. It depends really only on that which happens inside a person. I am grateful every day that I have you, and that makes me happy.

So, in bodily terms, their love ended. Owing to the war, and Bonhoeffer's arrest so soon after their engagement, they never were alone together as lovers. Yet, as the English poet John Donne wrote, love's mysteries in souls do grow, and without any doubt theirs continued to grow despite their cruel, and now final, separation.

I talked to Maria, and she told me that there were times she could be happy about the engagement and times when it was very hard to take because

I was getting closer and closer to a man whom I was not really getting closer to.

I went first to Flossenbürg. You could take a train to something like seven kilometers from the camp...I walked to Flossenbürg with a...rucksack full of clothing for Bonhoeffer. I knocked on the door and said I had been told by the Gestapo in Berlin that Bonhoeffer had been transferred to this concentration camp, that I had brought clothing and would they please deliver the clothing to him and return the old, so I could take care of it and wash it. I was met with great politeness. Of course, it didn't happen very often at the concentration camp that an eighteen-year-old girl walked up there for some errand...[so the guards] went through a believable effort in looking up his name.

At that point I didn't realize it but there were different lists. In one office they looked through one list, and since he wasn't on it, they said, "Why don't you go there?" And I went [to another office] and they looked through another long list. At that point I thought of list *A* or list *B*, or I don't know what, only later did I realize [that one of the lists was of those who had been executed.] But I was quite convinced when I was through – I would say I was a good two hours in that concentration camp – that they had made an honest effort to find him and that he wasn't there...And he wasn't, not yet, but eventually that is where he was executed.

I asked Maria what effect — if it is possible to express such a thing — Bonhoeffer's death had had on her and her life. She described the stages through which she had passed:

> At first, of course, it was very hard to accept the fact that he was dead, especially since I had never really been so close to him, and had had these long periods of not seeing him. It seemed like another big period of not seeing him. It was very hard to come to grips with the fact that this was indeed finished. I have continued to live my life looking at this as a great, great gift, a great…addition, a great enrichment of my life. Yet, on the other hand, it had its hard parts and it has been difficult, even to this very day it is sometimes difficult to accept that it is no longer there. Nothing else has really quite replaced it.

After the transfer to the Gestapo prison in Prinz-Albrecht-Strasse, Bonhoeffer was taken away from Berlin with a party of international prisoners. Perhaps it was just as well that he never came back. What, we may ask ourselves, would he have made of the city as it was resurrected after the war, with a macabre wall, dividing, not just two Berlins and two Germanys, but two worlds?

In taking his decision to return to Germany from America in the summer of 1939, Bonhoeffer had said: "Christians in Germany will face the terrible alternatives of either willing the defeat of their nation in order that Christian civilization may survive, or willing the victory

of their nation, and thereby destroying our civilization."
In the event, no such alternatives have arisen; their nation
and Christian civilization have both been submerged.

Berlin today – what a sad outcome of the defeat of
Hitler, an end towards which Bonhoeffer had chosen
to associate himself with such devious and violent purposes! In any case, he was spared the spectacle. From
Buchenwald he was taken with a party of prisoners to
Regensburg, and thence to Schönberg, traveling in a
preposterous vehicle fueled with wood, and in the cus-
tody of guards who seemed no less bewildered than the
prisoners themselves. At one point, when some village
girls asked for a lift, the guards told them they were
transporting a camera crew engaged in making a propaganda film. They spoke truer than they knew; in a
sense the drama of Bohoeffer's life and death, now ap-
proaching its climax, was to be for others.

Bonhoeffer and the other prisoners arrived at Schönberg on Saturday, April 7, 1945, and were lodged in the
village school. Then on the Sunday morning, all the prisoners, including Vassili Kokorin, said to be Molotov's
nephew, pressed Bonhoeffer to conduct a service. After
some hesitation, he agreed, taking as his text: "With his
stripes we are healed," and "Blessed be the God and
Father of our Lord Jesus Christ! By His great mercy
we have been born anew to a living hope through the

resurrection of Jesus Christ from the dead." Together they sang Luther's *Eine feste Burg*. An English survivor, Hugh Falconer, has said that it was an incomparable experience, which carried them all to great heights of spirituality.

Scarcely was the service over than two men appeared, and there was a shout: "Prisoner Bonhoeffer, get ready and come with us!" He knew what it meant and asked an Englishman who was present, Payne Best, to take a message from him to Bishop Bell of Chichester, to tell the Bishop that this was the end, but for him also the beginning of life, and that the ultimate victory of their cause – a universal Christian brotherhood rising above all national interest – was certain. Then Bonhoeffer was taken away.

Bishop Bell concluded his address at Bonhoeffer's memorial service in London:

> So now Dietrich has gone. Our debt to him, and to all others similarly murdered, is immense. He made the sacrifice of human prospects, of home, friends and career because he believed in God's vocation for his country, and refused to follow those false leaders who were the servants of the devil.
>
> Our Lord said, "Except a corn of wheat fall into the ground and die, it abideth alone; but if it die it bringeth forth much fruit. He that loveth his life shall lose it, and he that hateth his life in this world shall keep it unto life eternal." To our earthly view Dietrich is dead. Deep and unfathomable as our sorrow seems, let us comfort one another with these

words. For him and Klaus, and for the countless multitudes of their fellow victims through these terrible years of war, there is the resurrection from the dead; for Germany redemption and resurrection, if God pleases to lead the nation through men animated by his spirit, holy and humble and brave like him; for the Church, not only in that Germany which he loved, but the Church Universal, which was greater to him than nations, the hope of a new life. The blood of the martyrs is the seed of the Church.

Bonhoeffer arrived at the Flossenbürg prison camp on a Sunday evening and was at once summarily tried and condemned to death. His serene demeanor made a great impression on the prison doctor, who thus describes what happened:

> Through the half-open door in one room of the huts I saw Pastor Bonhoeffer, before taking off his prison garb, kneeling on the floor praying fervently to his God. I was most deeply moved by the way this lovable man prayed, so devout and so certain that God heard his prayer. At the place of execution, he again said a short prayer and then climbed the steps to the gallows, brave and composed. His death ensued after a few seconds. In almost fifty years that I worked as a doctor, I have hardly ever seen a man die so entirely submissive to the will of God.

As Bonhoeffer went to his death in Flossenbürg, five years of the monstrous buffooneries of war were drawing to a close. Hitler's Third Reich, which was to last for a thousand years, was soon to reach its ignominious and ruinous end. The liberators were moving in from the East and the West with bombs and tanks and guns and cigarettes and spam; the air was thick with rhetoric and cant.

Looking back now across the years, I ask myself where in that murky darkness any light shines. Not among the Nazis, certainly, nor among the liberators, who, as we now know, were to liberate no one and nothing. The rhetoric and the cant have mercifully been forgotten. What lives on is the memory of a man who died, not on behalf of freedom or democracy or a steadily rising Gross National Product, nor for any of the twentieth century's counterfeit hopes and desires, but on behalf of a Cross on which another man died two thousand years before. As on that previous occasion on Golgotha, so amidst the rubble and desolation of "liberated" Europe, the only victor is the man who died, as the only hope for the future lies in his triumph over death. There never can be any other victory or any other hope.

afterword

Since the programs whose scripts form this book were released for screening, they have been shown on various PBS channels in the United States, several times on the CBC network in Canada, and once on the BBC. Also — particularly pleasing to me — on numerous campuses. To judge by letters from viewers and reviews, the concept behind the programs — how throughout history God's spies mysteriously turn up as and when required, and can be fully recognized only in retrospect — would seem to have clearly emerged. For me personally, too, doing the commentaries has been a great clarification over and above identifying God's Spies and specifying their role in particular circumstances and at a particular time. It has made me grasp as never before that God has an inner strategic (as distinct from tactical) purpose for His creation, thereby enabling me to see through the Theater of the Absurd, which is what life seems to be, and into the Theater of Fearful Symmetry, which is what it is. Thus reality sorts itself out, like film coming into sync, and everything that exists, from the tiniest atom to the illimitable universe in which our tiny earth revolves, everything that happens, from the most trivial event to the most seemingly momentous, makes one pattern, tells one story, is comprehended in one prayer: Thy will be done.

M. M.

the author

Born in 1903 and educated at Cambridge University, Malcolm Muggeridge is often compared to G. K. Chesterton – both for his stylistic mastery of the English language, and for his defense of Christianity in an increasingly anti-Christian culture. Ironically, he himself was a vocal agnostic for most of his life, and embraced a personal faith only toward the end, something he formalized with his entry into the Catholic Church when he was eighty.

A foreign correspondent in Cairo, Moscow, Calcutta, and Washington, D.C., Muggeridge rose through the ranks to become one of England's most respected journalists. His career additionally spanned such roles as newspaper editor, major in the British Intelligence Corps, rector of Edinburgh University, and – most famously – editor of the British humor magazine *Punch*. By the 1960s and '70s, as a frequent guest on shows such as *Firing Line*, he was captivating radio and television audiences on both sides of the Atlantic with his sharp-tongued commentary and witty insights.

Muggeridge's articles are too numerous to describe here. His books include *Something Beautiful for God*, the classic biography of Mother Teresa of Calcutta often credited for introducing her to the western world; *Chronicles of Wasted Time*, a two-volume memoir hailed by the *Washington Post* as "one of the most fascinating and entertaining memoirs of our age"; *Jesus Rediscovered; Christ and the Media;* and *Confessions of a 20th Century Pilgrim*. He died in 1990 in Hastings, England.

The Gospel in Dostoyevsky

Edited by the Bruderhof
Woodcuts by Fritz Eichenberg

272 pages, softcover

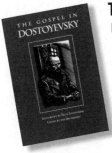

"If you are assailed by doubt, even total rejection of God, try Dostoyevsky. And don't be daunted by the fact that most of his books are fat. Start with this volume of power-laden excerpts." — *a reader*

An excellent introduction to one of the world's most important authors, this volume vividly reveals — as none of his novels can on their own — the common thread of the great God-haunted Russian's questioning faith. Drawn from *The Brothers Karamazov*, *The Idiot*, *Crime and Punishment*, and *The Adolescent*, the seventeen selections are each prefaced by an explanatory note.

Newcomers will find in these pages a rich, accessible sampling. Dostoyevsky devotees will be pleased to find some of the writer's deepest, most compelling passages in one volume. Full-page woodcuts by Fritz Eichenberg enhance the book.

Phyllis Tickle, *Publishers Weekly*
One of the best-conceived, most succinct and most useful Dostoyevsky readers…

Philip Yancey, *Christianity Today*
Grab it. Read it. And be careful: you may find yourself — as I did — scouring used bookstores for every obscure work of this incomparable writer.

To order, visit www.orbisbooks.com
or call 1-800-258-5838

Walk in the Light
And Twenty-Three Tales
Leo Tolstoy

360 pages, softcover

Uncluttered by the complexities of plot and character that daunt so many readers of the longer Russian masterpieces, Tolstoy's tales illumine eternal truths with forceful brevity. While inspired by a sense of spiritual certainty, their narrative quality, subtle humor, and visionary power lift them far above the common run of "religious" literature. Moralists purport to tell us what our lives should mean, and how we should live them. Tolstoy, on the other hand, has an uncanny gift for conveying what it means to be truly alive.

Contents:
A Talk among Leisured People • Walk in the Light • God Sees the Truth, but Waits • A Prisoner in the Caucasus • The Bear-Hunt • What Men Live By • A Spark Neglected Burns the House • Two Old Men • Where Love Is, God Is • The Story of Ivan the Fool • Evil Allures, but Good Endures • Little Girls Wiser than Men • Ilyas • The Three Hermits • The Imp and the Crust • How Much Land Does a Man Need? • A Grain as Big as a Hen's Egg • The Godson • The Repentant Sinner • The Empty Drum • The Coffeehouse of Surat • Too Dear! • Esarhaddon, King of Assyria • Work, Death, and Sickness: a Legend • Three Questions

Provocations
Spiritual Writings of Kierkegaard
Compiled and Edited by Charles E. Moore

464 pages, softcover

There are few authors as repeatedly quoted and consistently unread as Søren Kierkegaard. Kierkegaard himself is partly to blame for this: his style is dense, his thoughts complex. And yet embedded within his writings and journals are metaphors and truths so deep and vivid, they can overwhelm you with an almost blinding clarity.

Moore has done us an invaluable service by putting together arguably the most accessible and complete Kierkegaard volume to be published in decades. Here is a book for anyone who takes the search for authenticity seriously.

Divided into six sections, *Provocations* contains a little of everything from Kierkegaard's prodigious output, including his wryly humorous attacks on what he calls the "mediocre shell" of conventional Christianity, his brilliantly pithy parables, his amazing insights on the human condition, and his incisive attempts to dig through the fluff of theological jargon and clear a way for the basics: decisiveness, obedience, passion, and recognition of the truth.

Eugene Peterson, author, *Subversive Spirituality*
In a culture awash in religious silliness, Kierkegaard's bracing metaphors expose our mediocrities and energize us with a clarified sense of what it means to follow Jesus.

To order, visit www.orbisbooks.com
or call 1-800-258-5838